S.O.S. for Catholic Schools

S.O.S.
for Catholic Schools

*A Strategy for Future Service
to Church and Nation*

C. ALBERT KOOB AND
RUSSELL SHAW

Holt, Rinehart and Winston
NEW YORK   CHICAGO   SAN FRANCISCO

Published simultaneously in Canada by Holt, Rinehart and
Winston of Canada, Limited.

Library of Congress Catalog Card Number: 78-102147
First Edition

Designer: Ernst Reichl
SBN: 03-084521-1
Printed in the United States of America

Contents

S.O.S. for Catholic Schools

1 Catholic Education Today

FROM the outside, St. Patrick's school looks like everything that is wrong with American education. Built in 1890, it stands in a bleak, decaying neighborhood at the heart of a large midwestern city. Like many such educational relics it has the grim look of a fortress, as if its prime function were to imprison children rather than foster their experience of learning.

But from the inside St. Patrick's looks like everything that is right with American education. This, the visitor soon discovers, is not just another inner-city school, battling to keep its head above the swirling waves of ethnic tension and sociological change and still carry on the business of teaching. Rather, St. Patrick's is a place where many of the good things that educators write about and speak of as "innovation" have become a living reality.

St. Patrick's is a "lower school" (grades one through four), working in cooperation with a nearby parish school which serves as a "middle school" (grades five through eight). The cooperative arrangement permits a better use of faculty and facilities and thus makes for better education. The student population is mixed—white, Puerto Rican and black. The children are mostly disadvantaged—that is, they are poor. With all their handicaps, they have found in St. Patrick's a place where learning is not a dull or painful chore but a zestful challenge and a means of self-fulfillment. Gone from St. Patrick's is the rigid and arbitrary divi-

sion of students into grades, with all youngsters of a given
age assigned the same material at the same time whether or
not it happens to coincide with their skills. Several years
ago St. Patrick's went nongraded, and after a rather bumpy
shift of gears, the experiment is now in full and flexible operation.

Students are not passive spectators at St. Patrick's. Sometimes they do the teaching. Consider the role of Carlos, a
Puerto Rican whose native tongue is Spanish. In another
school, this fact plus Carlos' accent might have proved a
handicap both academically and socially. At St. Patrick's it
is an advantage, for Carlos has been drafted to tutor some of
his fellow students in Spanish and his self-esteem has risen
accordingly. St. Patrick's also makes creative use of adult
paraprofessionals—women who are not full-fledged teachers
but are able to shoulder some of the routine school tasks,
thus freeing the faculty for thinking, planning and extra
work with individual students.

St. Patrick's is a Catholic school. But it is a far cry from
the old stereotype, the parochial school where rigid discipline and rote were taken for granted. In fact, St. Patrick's
is not a parish school at all, but one that is independently incorporated, recognized and functioning as a "community"
school: that is, it accepts students from the surrounding
neighborhood without regard for their religious affiliation,
and is thus obliged to be responsive to the entire community. The sisters and lay teachers who staff St. Patrick's are
conscious of doing something new and creative, and a spirit
of excitement and adventure has infected the entire faculty.
Its members are firmly committed to the idea of Catholic
education, but not to the time-honored mold in which it has
been cast.

A few years ago St. Patrick's had a decision to make. The
white Catholic population of the parish that had built and
maintained the school had largely moved away. A new pop-

ulation, black, Puerto Rican and lower middle class, had taken their place. The school could struggle to go on as it was, a "parish" institution that served a diminishing clientele. Or it could deliberately choose for itself an experimental role—one based on community service and educational innovation—and thus hope to have meaning for the future. St. Patrick's opted for the latter approach, and the results to date have been gratifying.

They have been gratifying, too, in hundreds of other Catholic schools in communities throughout the country. St. Patrick's is a model in one sense—its willingness to confront changing times and adopt new approaches—but in another sense it is inimitable, just as any good school must be if it is to respond to the particular needs of the community it serves. More and more Catholic schools are recognizing this fact and seeking to adjust themselves to it.

It would be a mistake, however, to suppose that willingness to experiment and innovate is the whole story of Catholic education today. Although it is everywhere undergoing change, the motive force behind that change varies widely from place to place. In some places, change has come as a result of effective planning; an example is the move toward setting up lay boards of trustees in Catholic colleges. In others, change is occurring as the panic-stricken response to more or less unanticipated pressures, and has meant the precipitous dropping of grades and even the closing of schools in some dioceses. In still other instances, thought and planning have preceded change, but it is possible that many important consequences of significant decisions have not been fully assessed—for example, the rapid growth of parish and diocesan lay boards of education.

Although change of many different kinds is taking place, the most conspicuous has been the decline during the last several years in the number of Catholic elementary and secondary schools (by about 3 per cent in 1968–69 from the year before), and in the number of students in these schools (by about 5 per cent in the last school year to just under five million).

Change, however, is not synonymous with decline. With proper planning and execution, Catholic education in America can be strengthened and deepened as a result of having to adjust to new times and situations. The danger is that change will come about without adequate preparation and coordination. Even when effective planning for change occurs in one sector of the Catholic educational system, it can be vitiated by ineffective planning—or none at all—in another. In organization, Catholic education is still rigidly segmented; there is an extremely high degree of separatism among individual parishes, dioceses, religious communities, and other agencies and groups involved. This is true even though various sectors of the Catholic educational system are in fact highly interdependent and becoming more so. Bad planning by a particular religious community, for instance, can damage Catholic education in a score of dioceses; dropping grades in elementary schools will have an eventual impact on Catholic education at the secondary level and even higher—to say nothing of the immediate impact on public education at the same level. And lack of intelligent financial planning for Catholic education in one diocese can damage the relations of dioceses throughout an entire state with government officials who administer state and federal aid to education.

Since changes in Catholic education also affect public education, public officials in a particular city or state must anticipate the future course of Catholic education in order to do their own planning intelligently. This is particularly true in the many urban areas where Catholic schools account for a large part of the total school enrollment. Intelligent planning for change in Catholic education will be a boon to public education and government; a chaotic lunging about as one or another aspect of crisis clamors for attention will be a disaster for all of American education.

1 Research

If there is to be planning for change in Catholic education, there is an obvious need for research as a prerequisite for decision-making. In their *Statement on Catholic Schools* of November 16, 1967, the U. S. Catholic Bishops declared:

Like our colleagues in this teaching apostolate, we too do not want to go beyond our means, nor to dilute quality for the sake of quantity nor to expend excessive resources on one kind of education with consequent neglect of other forms. We therefore acknowledge the immediate need for more research to evaluate our present endeavors, to project our future responsibilities, and to make a thorough inventory of our resources in personnel and finance.

An impressive start has been made in recent years toward remedying the truly appalling lack of data about Catholic education. The national studies of Catholic education conducted several years ago at the University of Notre Dame and the National Opinion Research Center made important contributions to knowledge of the situation as it was in the early 1960s. The Notre Dame study, *Catholic Schools in Action,* provided massive statistical documentation on Catholic schools, their teachers and students. The NORC study (*The Education of Catholic Americans*) delved into the social, academic and religious "outcomes" of Catholic schooling. Research and self-study are now moving to the diocesan level as various dioceses undertake programs designed to assess available resources and draft workable plans for the future.

Nevertheless, much more work is needed on a continuing basis, as has often been pointed out by officials in the gov-

ernment and in public education. The national profile assembled by the Notre Dame and NORC studies requires
elaboration, as well as constant updating in this period of
rapid transition. Many questions about the outcomes of
Catholic educational programs remain unanswered. And
the isolated diocesan studies of Catholic education, important as they are, do not provide the data required for intelligent planning and decision-making at the state, regional
and national levels, where planning and decisions are becoming increasingly necessary.

2 *Attitudes*

The ferment in the Catholic Church as a whole extends
to Catholic education. It seems clear that Catholic schools
can no longer expect the blind loyalty that prevailed in the
not too distant past, at least among a majority of Catholics.
It is also clear that many Catholic lay people are disturbed
by what they regard as the present deficiencies of Catholic
education: alleged academic weaknesses; too little emphasis
on new theological trends in the Church—or too much emphasis on these same trends; too little emphasis on racial
and social justice—or too much; too much old-fashioned
discipline—or too much permissiveness; the fact that their
children are as likely to be taught by lay teachers as by religious.

The attitudes of many of the clergy and religious have
also shifted. Some pastors and curates are reluctant to assume the burden of fund-raising for parochial schools. Some
sisters, who feel stifled in parochial schools, are looking—
and moving—toward public education, the inner city, and
other diversified forms of service.

As such shifts in attitudes toward Catholic education become more widespread, their effects will be felt in the com-

position of the Catholic school teaching force, in decisions to close existing schools or to open new ones, in the financial support of Catholic education by the Catholic public, and in other important areas.

Generally speaking, it seems safe to describe the present attitude of the Catholic public toward Catholic schools as "friendly but selective." That is to say, all other things being equal, most Catholics will choose to send their children to a Catholic school. But where other things are *not* equal— where, for instance, a particular school is regarded as too far away, too expensive, academically inferior to a nearby public school, or simply not the "right" school for a particular child—then today's Catholic parent will feel little or no hesitation about sending his children to a public school or a non-Catholic private one. There is still a receptive clientele for Catholic schooling, but its attitude is no longer uncritical.

3　Policy-Making

Radical changes in the policy-making structure of Catholic colleges are now apparent, but the same is true at the elementary and secondary levels as well.

In the past, policy-making was centralized in the hands of the bishops and religious superiors. Today, however, many of them prefer not to exercise this function unilaterally, feeling both that they lack the necessary expertise and that ideological currents in the Church and in American society now call for a participatory approach.

At the same time, Catholic parents and Catholic school teachers are becoming increasingly restive under the procedures that have prevailed up to now. Both groups want a larger voice in educational decisions. And Catholic school superintendents seem to be undergoing their own crisis of identity. The superintendent is uncertain whether he is an ecclesiastical official or an educational one, or both (and if both, he is uncertain how to reconcile the two roles); he does not know whether he works for the bishop or the community or both (and again, if for both, how he is to reconcile the built-in tensions of this situation).

The Catholic board of education movement is a major new element in this picture. Some 4,500 such boards are now functioning on the parish and diocesan levels. They vary widely in composition, in the manner in which their members are selected, and in their authority, which may be anything from advisory to jurisdictional. In the estimate of many, jurisdictional boards, through which true control of educational policy is placed in the hands of the sponsoring community, now represent the best long-range hope for the future of Catholic education. Yet their own future is by no means clear. Some Catholic educators strongly urge that the boards take over, with little or no modification, the pattern of public-school boards. Others note that the public board of education is less than ideal as a policy-making body, and urge that Catholic education be cautioned accordingly.

4 *Finances*

Ernest Bartell, C.S.C., compares the financial setup of the American Catholic Church, and especially of Catholic education, to that of an underdeveloped country; a lack of hard fiscal data, he observes, is one of the basic similarities. Literally no one now knows just how much it costs in the United States to operate Catholic schools and the Church's other educational programs. Still less does anyone know what it will cost in the future. And least of all does anyone know what a substantial redirection of the thrust of Catholic education—by introducing, for example, a large, high-quality Catholic school "presence" in the inner city—can be expected to cost.

Nevertheless, it is certain that Catholic education is already very expensive and will, if it is maintained in anything like its present dimensions, become even more so in the future. This is certain to come about, if for no other reason, because of the increasing proportion of lay teachers in Catholic schools. The likelihood of greater militancy on the part of teachers' associations and unions only adds to the problem.

At the same time, the current means of financing Catholic education—i.e., by fixed charges for tuition and fees—are recognized as inadequate and essentially unjust, since the burden placed on low-income families is disproportionately heavy. There is dissatisfaction, too, with the lack of expertise in planning and budgeting among Catholic educational administrators. Although major efforts to develop new sources of income, chiefly from government aid, are under way, it is far from clear whether that income will be large enough or come soon enough to rescue Catholic education from its current plight.

More and more is being learned, however—often through painful experience—about the saving to the American taxpayer represented by the Catholic school system. Back in 1958, Roger Freeman estimated that if all children attending nonpublic schools had been enrolled in public schools in 1940, public school expenditures would have been approximately $244 million higher. By 1955–56 this figure had risen to $1.8 billion, and Freeman predicted that by 1970 the figure would be close to $4 billion. For the most part the American educational community and the American public have yet to reflect on the implications for the public schools, and thus for the taxpayer, of the fiscal crisis in Catholic schools. If Freeman is correct, the closing of all nonpublic schools would increase the taxpayer's bill for public schooling by about $4 billion a year. To be sure, not all nonpublic schools are going to close. But many already have done so, and more presumably will in the years immediately ahead, so that what is now commonly seen as a "Catholic" problem may rather soon begin to be seen—as it should be—as a problem for American education generally.

5 *Personnel*

The size and the composition of the Catholic school teaching force are changing dramatically. During the school year of 1957–58, lay teachers numbered 35,129 out of a full-time total of 147,330. In 1967–68, lay teachers numbered 90,066 in a total of 206,959.

In part, the shift in the ratio of lay to religious teachers is a result of the relatively slight increase in the number of religious teachers over this ten-year span, as compared with the number of schools and of pupils. The current dropoff in priestly and religious vocations suggests, however, that the ratio will continue to shift, and that in the future it will reflect not a growth in the number of Catholic schools but an absolute decline in the number of religious.

Not much information, unfortunately, is now available about the sources of supply for the Catholic teaching force of the future. Facts about the current trend in priestly and religious vocations are difficult to obtain, and when available they are often colored by emotional bias. Yet without such information, intelligent planning for the future of Catholic education is scarcely possible. It is, for instance, vastly important for financial planning to know (or at least make an intelligent guess) about whether in, say, the year 1980, laymen will constitute 50 per cent, 60 per cent or 80 per cent of the teaching force in Catholic elementary and secondary schools. It is also important to know whether religious teachers will be concentrated in certain congregations and certain sections of the country, and, if so, in which ones.

6 *Structures*

A variety of innovations—which for convenience may be lumped under the catch-all term "structures"—are now being, or soon will be, introduced into Catholic education. These include programs for sharing facilities and services with public schools; teaching by educational technology; pre-school and adult education; non-school religious education (as, for example, in catechetical centers, ecumenical or otherwise); special programs for disadvantaged children and adults; and instructional methods such as team teaching and individual instruction.

The long-range implications of these structures for Catholic education have yet to be assessed. What impact, for instance, will educational technology have on the Catholic education of the future? How do home learning centers fit into the pattern of Catholic education? Again, if there were to be a major thrust by Catholic education into the inner city, what special training and retraining of Catholic school teachers would be necessary? Would the existing physical plant of inner-city Catholic parishes be adequate, or would substantial new facilities be needed? What inner-city programs that have proved themselves in practice can become models for Catholic educators?

Similar questions can be asked about all of the other "structures" mentioned above. Unless they are asked and answered, there is a real danger that at some point in the future Catholic education may find itself irrevocably committed to programs and facilities that no longer correspond to educational needs and opportunities.

The authors of this book do not pretend to have answers to all of these questions. Their aim is, rather, to suggest certain attitudes and procedures—ways of looking at things and of doing things—that will be essential if the answers (which, one hopes, will soon be available) are to be used wisely in making decisions about Catholic education. Several themes will recur in what follows: the necessity of opening up Catholic schools to cooperation with other educational programs, both church-related and not, and to the service of new publics in addition to (but not in place of) those they have traditionally accommodated; the need for new, community-oriented, participatory decision-making; the theme of "accountability"—in regard to money and all other aspects of the Catholic school program; and, finally, what the authors see as the imperative requirement—that Catholic schools keep the emphasis on excellence, both academic and apostolic, in whatever they do, and accept all the consequences of the choice—even if that means less emphasis on total numbers, either of schools or of students.

Let there be no doubt about the matter: we believe that Catholic schools do have a role to play in American society and in the Catholic Church. This role seems to us indispensable, but it can no longer be taken for granted. Just as historic changes have occurred—and at an accelerating rate—in the Catholic Church and American society during recent years, so the special function of Catholic schools in Church and society has changed and needs now to be redefined. As Bishop Ernest J. Primeau of Manchester, New Hampshire, has observed, anyone concerned with the well-being of Catholic education today is confronted with the challenge of formulating reasons for the continued existence of a Catholic school system in the United States. The issue is important, not because Catholic schools ought no longer to exist, but because of the excellent reasons why these schools *should* exist—reasons that deserve to be spelled out. Some of these reasons will become apparent in the course of this book, but their elaboration is not its only aim. Equally important, we hope to show what must be done if American Catholic schools are to continue to be a vital and effective force in the Church and the nation.

Pressures on Catholic Education

Catholic schools do not exist in a vacuum—nor even, any longer, in a ghetto. One of the mistakes often made by those who discuss them is to speak as if they did. Catholic schools influence, and in turn are influenced by, what happens in the Church, the nation and the world. In order to understand the current pressures on Catholic schools, it is necessary to understand the pressures now being exerted on education generally.

Ours has been called the Age of Anxiety, the Age of Technology, the Age of the Layman, and so on. With no little justice it can also be called the Age of Education. It is an age notable for the ubiquity of education, the demand for it, and the need for it. Consider the demand. A few years ago one of the authors of this book participated in a study tour of Peru with a group of American educators. During that visit, the President of Peru remarked to the group that some 50 per cent of his nation's children did not have access to any school at all. He stressed his own and his country's determination to make up this deficiency, and said he was prepared to recruit teachers of any nationality and any ideology —democratic, socialist or communist—that could handle the job. The statement may come as a shock to North American ears, but it should not. Throughout the world today, forward-looking national leaders are convinced that education is the key to progress, and they are determined to supply it at whatever cost.

This should come as no surprise to anyone with a sense of history. Indeed, education has always been regarded as essential for those who want to move up the social and economic ladder. Though certain romantic humanists may deplore the fact—those of the sort for whom education consists exclusively of the disinterested pursuit of knowledge for its own sake—realism compels a recognition that knowledge is power: power to change society, power to change the world, power first of all to change the conditions of one's own life.

Think of the late Middle Ages. It is often said that the invention of gunpowder was one of the chief factors leading to the collapse of the feudal system in Western Europe. The peasant who went into battle armed with a primitive musket was, as it turned out, more than a match for the armored knight on horseback. Thus, it is said, the clatter of armored knights unhorsed became the death knell of medieval society. And so it may have been—in part. But an even larger factor in the end of the Middle Ages, in the estimate of many, was Gutenberg's invention of movable type and the impetus it gave to literacy. The peasant with a musket may have been formidable, but even more formidable was the peasant who could read. When education became accessible to masses of people, the foundations of the rigid hierarchical structure of society had been undermined, and it was only a matter of time before the French Revolution would definitively seal the fact.

To talk of the Middle Ages and the French Revolution may suggest that all this occurred only in the distant past. As a matter of fact, the same process—the social ascent of underprivileged groups through education—is taking place today on an unprecedented scale. The Harlem pupil enrolled in a Head Start program and the Ethiopian village dweller learning to read from a Peace Corpsman are repeating a pattern that has reached global dimensions since the time of Gutenberg. They are engaged in a learning process that enables them to exercise a never before dreamed-of degree of control over their lives and their surroundings.

The pursuit of individual and national development is only one of the factors that have made this an Age of Education. Technology is another. Science has made it possible for man to shape and control his environment in ways that, fifty years ago, few besides readers of the novels of Jules Verne and H. G. Wells had envisioned. But the body of scientific knowledge that has been built up in this short time is so fantastically complex and so specialized that only a highly structured system of formal education can possibly codify it and pass it on to new generations.

But even while technology and technological education have grown and prospered, men have begun to concern themselves more and more feverishly with questions about the meaning of the universe and human life in it. This, too, has imposed new pressures on education. In a world that appeared stable, even static, many things could be taken for granted. There was a consensus that the answers to the big questions—who is man? what is he doing here? what is life all about?—had been found long ago, and that if anyone had doubts he could simply look them up. For better or worse, all this has changed today. With all his achievements and discoveries, modern man is radically unsure of himself. He looks in many places for answers to his questions, and education is one of those places.

It is against this background that Catholic schools today must find their role and rationale. When, a century ago, Catholic schools were being established in the United States on a massive scale, the reasons why were clear enough (even if not universally accepted). "In days like ours," went a statement by the Third Plenary Council of Baltimore in 1884, "when error is so pretentious and aggressive, every one needs to be as completely armed as possible with sound knowledge—not only the clergy, but the people also that they may be able to withstand the noxious influences of popularized irreligion." Catholic schools, then, were essentially a defensive response, a way of arming the Catholic people against forces regarded as inimical to their faith.

Prudently enough, the bishops assembled at Baltimore spoke only of "popularized irreligion" as the enemy. In fact, however, the problem went further than that. As is now well known, the public schools of the time reflected a strongly Protestant orientation and were regarded by many of their strongest supporters as in reality Protestant institutions which could serve, among other things, to wean Catholic children away from the pernicious superstitions of Rome.

The Catholic school system in the United States was therefore established in response to what Catholic leadership viewed as a crisis. As wave upon wave of Catholic immigrants arrived from Ireland, Germany and other countries, the Church in America faced the desperate challenge of providing for their religious needs—and in particular for the religious education of their children. As Father Neil McCluskey, S.J., puts it, "The predominantly immigrant and working-class Catholic group had little choice but to put their youngsters into the public schools where, from a Catholic point of view, the religious atmosphere was often intolerable. Leakage from the Church was serious. Hundreds of thousands of Catholic children were growing up in almost complete ignorance of their heritage of faith."

Were Catholic schools the appropriate response to this situation? The question is almost frivolous. The leaders and people of the American Church in the nineteenth century were faced with the staggering challenge of keeping the faith alive within a hard-pressed immigrant group surrounded by a suspicious and hostile majority. The only reasonable criterion by which to judge this effort is its success in meeting the need of the time, and the only realistic judgment is that it was a success indeed. The size and vigor of the Church in America today—for all its easily-enumerated faults and failings and weaknesses—bear this out.

Paradoxically, however, the relative success of the Church in America is a cause, or at least a condition, of the problems Catholic schools now face. When an institution or a group is under siege, there is little disposition on anyone's part to engage in self-examination and self-criticism. "Rally round the flag" is the only meaningful motto, just as it is the almost universal response. But the Catholic Church in America has today emerged from its long state of siege, and in the new atmosphere of acceptance it has found the emotional and intellectual resources for a searching re-examination of its goals and programs, including those encompassed by Catholic education.

Much of the criticism directed at Catholic education, and specifically at Catholic schools, has been valid and useful. One thinks, for example, of the objections raised in the mid-1950's by Monsignor John Tracy Ellis and others, who pointed to academic deficiencies in the Catholic school program and thereby began a process of self-examination and reform that is still continuing. More recently, however, such reasoned and valuable criticism has tended to be replaced by vague uneasiness and unfocused hostility. Surveying the current state of Catholic education, one is reminded of John W. Gardner's description of "twentieth century institutions . . . caught in a savage crossfire between uncritical lovers and unloving critics":

On the one side, those who loved their institutions tended to smother them in an embrace of death, loving their rigidities more than their promise, shielding them from life-giving criticism. On the other side, there arose a breed of critics without love, skilled in demolition but untutored in the arts by which human institutions are nurtured and strengthened and made to flourish.

Catholic schools today clearly cannot afford to adopt a policy of unbending rigidity and resistance to change. Even supposing they could survive by doing so (which is doubtful), they would be remiss in their duty. The critics of Catholic schools are quite right in drawing attention to an imbalance in allocating Church resources for education. The solution, however, does not lie in closing down the schools and thus dissipating the resources, but rather in opening them up, making them dynamic centers of Christian education with the aim of serving the total community. It would, in our estimation, be a calamity for Catholic schools if either the defenders of the institutional status quo or the advocates of institutional demolition had their way.

Part of the problem for Catholic schools has been the widely held expectation that they should do everything public schools do, and provide religious education besides. This expectation has good aspects as well as bad. On the plus side, pressures on the Catholic schools to achieve educational excellence—pressures generated by the public schools' striving to uphold standards of their own—have had the good effect of keeping Catholic educators on their toes. A reasonable infusion of the competitive spirit is as healthy for them as for anyone else.

On a deeper level, too, there are sound reasons for the effort made by Catholic educators to provide a parallel to the offerings of public education. The "permeation" concept—the idea that religious values should be part and parcel of even the most "secular" subject—does have a certain validity, even if it has often been pushed too far. On the grounds of religious principle alone, it may not be easy to justify the existence of, say, Catholic dental schools; but a very respectable case can be made for scientific research and professional education under religious auspices. If religious values have any relation to the sciences and professional disciplines (and we are assuming that they do), then it is perfectly reasonable that a dialogue between the two should take place to a great extent within schools. This does not presume the existence of a "Catholic" mathematics or a "Catholic" sociology. It does presume that religion has something specific to say to the mathematician and the sociologist that can best be said within a school under its own auspices.

But the tendency of Catholic education to mimic public education also has less happy aspects. For one thing, it has led to an *a priori* commitment to Catholic education at every level, from pre-school through graduate school. This commitment may very well be necessary and desirable. The point here, however, is that up until the recent past its necessity and desirability have been assumed, not demonstrated. A commitment on the scale of this one deserves much more examination than it has received thus far among American Catholics.

Even worse, the decision that Catholic schools should be just like the public schools, only more so, has resulted in efforts to provide all the gadgets and gimmicks that sometimes make a modern American school look more like a three-ring circus than an institution of learning. Was there a tendency in public education to build bigger schools? Then Catholics would build bigger schools too. Were the public schools supporting interscholastic athletic programs? Then the Catholic schools would have such programs too (although Catholic school teams would usually compete in their own leagues, since ecumenism had not yet touched the realm of sports). Did the public schools have uniformed marching bands? Then, come hell and high water, the Catholic schools would have them too, and never mind the expense!

However one may feel about this sort of educational keeping up with the Joneses, no one should be surprised by it. It reflects what has been up to now almost a total consensus among American Catholics as to what Catholic schools should be doing. At one time it appeared essential to many first- and second-generation American Catholics that their schools match the public schools, especially in the external trappings of education. The schools were one more extension of the spirit of triumphalism—a response to the demand that Catholic bands be bigger and Catholic football teams be brawnier. And if the spirit has changed to some degree today, the pressure on Catholic schools to compete with public schools in all things curricular and extracurricular not only remains, but is if anything stronger. Educational excellence—or what is thought of as excellence—has become a status symbol for the affluent, and woe betide the suburban Catholic school whose educational offering is reputed to lack quality, as "quality" is defined in suburbia.

Further complicating life for American educators in general and for Catholic educators in particular is the longstanding habit in America of looking to the schools for many non-academic services under the rubric of "life adjustment." If it were simply a matter of having teenage boys and girls taught to drive a car by high school instructors rather than by their fathers, no one could object very much: actually, the trained instructor may do a better job. What causes trouble is the tendency of many parents to expect the schools to take over from themselves the task of forming their children in virtue and good citizenship. In this, to be sure, schools have an important role—indeed, a vital one—but the home remains the principal source and shaper of such values. What the school can do is to reinforce values already held by offering a structured intellectual rationale, along with practical experience of living out these values in a larger community than the home. But the home is still at the core of the process. Many of the alleged failures of the schools to develop high standards and sound character among young people reflect rather a failure on the part of parents, and the blame attached to the schools arises from a basic confusion about the process of socialization.

Although the school is expected generally to be all things to all men, that expectation is strongest in regard to religious education. Catholic parents have traditionally sent their children to Catholic schools on the assumption that they would there learn what it meant to *be* a Catholic. But today's Catholic school is confronted with a major crisis in religious education. The winds of change are blowing fiercely in the Catholic Church, and in recent years the disturbance has penetrated the classrooms of Catholic schools. The doubt and confusion that trouble many areas of Catholic life are nowhere felt more strongly than in Catholic education. Uncertainty produces an unfavorable climate for instruction. Ask any Catholic school teacher which subject is the hardest to teach today, and the answer is almost certain to be: religion.

A few consolations may be suggested: that, as has often been said before, the present moment is one of transition in the Church, and so things are sure to get better (although they may first become a good deal worse); that the fundamentals of Christianity do remain and can be taught, or at least taught about; and that (cold comfort perhaps), difficult though it may be to live and still more to teach in an era like this one, the experience can also be immensely stimulating. Out of the current turmoil in the Church, there has emerged one concept that Catholic school people should seize with joy because it gives meaning to their present frustration. This is the vision of the People of God. If the ideal of "integrating" religion into the Catholic school program means anything, it should mean this vision of the Christian community underlying every aspect of Catholic education. The school is a place where the child not only learns about, but learns to *live*, Christianity. Here, in embryo, is the central justification for the sacrifice and hardship that go into building and sustaining Catholic schools. For although the reality of the People of God can surely be seen and lived elsewhere, it is just as surely essential that it be seen and experienced within the school, which consumes so much of the time and emotional energy of young people at a crucial period of their growth.

This does not contradict what has already been said about the home as the primary source of values. Values are established in the home, but they are practiced in the community—and for young people the "community" means, to a great extent, the school. So far as the religious formation of the young is concerned, it is simply not possible to separate home and school, or to imagine that one can do a satisfactory job without the other. In a different and simpler society, where family ties were stronger and more durable, the formation and reinforcement of values could perhaps have been the task of the family, aided by the parish. But contemporary America is not that kind of society. The world of the modern American child between the ages of seven and seventeen is to a great extent the world of the school. This fact is surely a reason in itself for the continued existence of Catholic schools. But it is not one to encourage complacency among Catholic educators.

Of an almost endless list of problems and opportunities facing Catholic schools today, at least two more call for mention here and for extended discussion in a later chapter. One is the expanding role of laymen in the Church. The other is the influence of ecclesiastical patterns—in particular, the traditional territorial parish—carried over from a bygone age.

The American Catholic Church has now lived for more than a century under the shadow of lay trusteeism—that unpleasant episode in nineteenth-century Catholicism which found bishops and laymen frequently locked in combat over control of the temporal and even the spiritual affairs of the Church. One result of the controversy over trusteeism was that laymen were forced into a subordinate role, treated as inferior but potentially dangerous subjects, to be guided and controlled from above by clergy and religious.

Though the scars left by the battle over lay trusteeism are, fortunately, fading, they have not yet disappeared, and are especially evident in Catholic education. Take the case of the lay teacher in a Catholic school. Until the very recent past (and in many places even today), he or she was only grudgingly accepted, and always with the understanding, first, that the position had been granted only until such time as a religious could be found to take the job, and second, that no questions would be raised about working conditions and salary (however shockingly low), and no effort made to have an effective voice in the making of school policy. As for the notion that a layman might be principal of a Catholic elementary or secondary school, or president of a Catholic college—not only was it unheard of, but if voiced it would have been tantamount to heresy.

Consider, too, the relations of the Catholic parent with the Catholic school. No institution in America has said more often and more loudly than the Catholic Church that parents have the primary right in regard to the education of their children. But for years this meant no more than the "right" to surrender their children to Catholic schools and then gracefully withdraw from the scene. The parent who questioned some policy or procedure of the Catholic school was often told in no uncertain terms, "If you don't like the way we do things here, you can send your child to the public school!" Catholic educators enjoyed all the advantages of the seller in a sellers' market, and the way in which they exploited those advantages was, to say the least, not always tactful.

Today much of this has changed. Lay teachers are here to stay (90,000 of them in Catholic elementary and secondary schools in 1967-68). We are beginning to have lay principals and lay college presidents. Lay-dominated school boards (parish and diocesan) and lay boards of trustees (college) are growing in numbers and influence. But since no one—not the bishops or the pastors, not the principals or the teachers or the parents—is quite sure of himself in this new situation, tensions are inevitable. We shall take a look at some of these tensions in a later chapter.

We shall have more to say, too, about the parish structure and the way in which it has sometimes hindered the logical and efficient development of Catholic schools. It is enough to note here that, although in some places Catholic schools should certainly be parochial, there is today no reason to suppose that the entire Catholic educational enterprise (at least on the elementary level) should be organized on that basis. Continued insistence on the parish as the natural unit for formal education, as well as for educational financing and administration, has already put a heavy strain on Catholic education and could very soon bring it to the breaking point.

If Catholic education and Catholic schools in America are to continue to serve the Church and society, then a radical change of attitude and of method is necessary. To some degree the change is already under way. Foresighted people concerned about the future of Catholic education—bishops, superintendents, religious superiors, religious and lay educators, pastors and parents—have begun the work of reorganization and reorientation. This book is not simply a vision of what might be done but a reflection of what is already happening. The steps now being taken in some places must, however, be taken in many others as well. Only thus can the change now occurring in Catholic education be ultimately a change for the better.

2 Who Speaks for Catholic Education?

THE diocese of Midwest City has a choice to make. Should it build a new seminary (at present it sends its candidates for the priesthood to a major seminary in another state, which it shares with three other dioceses), or should it establish well-staffed, well-equipped Newman centers at three non-Catholic universities within its boundaries? Since the diocese does not have the money and manpower to do both, how is the choice to be made between these alternatives? Where is the voice of Catholic education in such circumstances?

Down at the parochial level, suburban St. Mary's parish is also facing a choice. The parish has been told by the community of nuns who staff St. Mary's School that two fewer teaching sisters will be assigned there next fall. Moreover, St. Mary's is feeling competitive pressure; an academically excellent public school in the neighborhood is becoming more and more attractive to Catholic parents. The parish knows it will have to raise tuition to hire lay teachers to take the nuns' places, and the rise in tuition will probably cause quite a few children to enroll in the public school. At the same time, St. Mary's has become aware that the schools of two other neighboring parishes are facing similar problems. Will St. Mary's go it alone (the customary procedure up to now), and either struggle to maintain its eight-grade parochial school or else make some such unilateral (and probably ill-advised) adjustment as dropping the first two

grades from the school? Or will the parish look beyond its
borders and arrive at a cooperative arrangement with its sister parishes? Under such a program, the first four grades
might be taught in one parish, the second four in another,
and the educational plant of the third be used to house a catechetical center for children and adults, conducted by a lay
and religious faculty drawn from all three parishes.

Neither the diocese of Midwest City nor St. Mary's parish
faces an automatically simple choice. If a wise decision is to
be made, it must be preceded by a competent survey of financial and demographic issues as well as strictly educational
ones. Furthermore, if it is to command the support needed
for success, it should not be made unilaterally by a single
authority, but should grow out of consultation and policy
formation involving all those who will be affected by the
eventual decisions, including the clergy, the sisters, the
Catholic laity and, most likely, representatives of the non-
Catholic community.

To set up a structure for this collegial process of arriving
at a decision is not an easy matter, simply because this is not
the way things have been done in Catholic education up to
now. Thus, before attempting an answer to the question
that is the title of this chapter—who speaks for Catholic education?—it is necessary to recognize that the question has
no answer, or, at any rate, none that is single, simple, and
neatly categorized. Despite lingering notions that the
Church is a monolith, a whole chorus of voices today
"speak" for Catholic education, and often each one seems to
be saying something different.

In another time and place, this might be an advantage;
even today, within limits, it is not a bad thing. Diversity has
value, in Catholic education as in other fields, and a multiplicity of attitudes and ideas has much to recommend it.
Any plea for unification, cooperation and coordination in
Catholic education should go hand in hand with a second
plea for flexibility and openness to alternatives.

Nevertheless, the present situation in the Catholic schools goes dangerously beyond the point of fruitful diversity, extending, at least in some places, to inefficiency and near chaos. Anyone surveying the Catholic educational scene today finds confusion, conflict, imbalance and even, it can at least be argued, gross inequity in the distribution of human and material resources. This being so, Catholics must stop congratulating themselves on the diversity of their educational system and begin to seek ways of planning and acting jointly with other individuals and organizations.

This is not to suggest that problems can be solved by a simple rearrangement of squares on an organizational chart. One thing is certain, however: the problems are not going to be solved without radical reorganization. Old structures for policy-making and for action are no longer adequate. In the next few years crucial decisions are going to be made about the future of Catholic education, decisions that in all likelihood will establish the patterns that are to prevail for decades to come. An efficient policy-making machinery is essential if these decisions are to be made wisely.

Possibly the most crucial task now facing Catholic education is that of establishing priorities. Almost everyone agrees that it would be wonderful if there were enough money, teachers, buildings and equipment to cover every possible contingency, from pre-school education to Church-sponsored special courses for the elderly. But that is not the way things are. Catholic education in many places is in a state of acute financial crisis; the supply of teachers is barely adequate to current needs; the expense of constructing, equipping and maintaining schools in the manner called for by modern education is soaring.

Moreover, just at a time when human and material resources seem to be caught in an ever tightening squeeze, Catholic educators have become conscious of pressing new responsibilities. (Possibly one should not really call them "new," but the widespread awareness of them certainly is.)

Catholic education can no longer be considered synonymous with the parochial school. A new public (or, at least, a newly articulate one) stands in need of what Catholic education can offer. It includes the poor and disadvantaged, both children and adults, whose plight is a reproach to the Christian conscience; the mass of Catholic grade and high school children who do not attend Catholic schools and whose religious education is very often neglected; Catholic adults bewildered by developments in the post-conciliar Church; and the million or so Catholic college students on non-Catholic campuses.

Add to these new responsibilities confronting Catholic education its antecedent responsibility to the five and a half million young people now enrolled in Catholic schools and colleges (a responsibility too easily ignored by some of those who see "phasing out" the schools as the solution to all problems), and one is faced with a challenging though not necessarily irreconcilable dilemma: how can Catholic education meet new demands when it is already hard pressed to maintain its present dimensions?

To this agonizing question, the establishment of a unified and coherent mechanism of policy-making is clearly part of the answer. Later we shall examine the question of how such a mechanism is to be put in operation. First however, we are compelled to underline the difficulties that continued postponement of this step will entail—not out of any morbid pleasure in their contemplation but for the very sound reason that unless the urgency of the matter is understood, action to deal with it is likely to be delayed too long.

Up to the present, Catholic educational programs—the school, the Confraternity of Christian Doctrine, adult education, Newman organizations and so on—have for the most part operated in uncommunicative isolation from one another. Each has begged, battled and bargained for whatever share of the available resources it could lay its hands on.

The time has long since passed when this sort of haphazard, every-man-for-himself approach could be considered acceptable. Catholic education is not an exercise in empire-building, however nobly motivated, but service by and to the People of God. Like anyone who performs a service, Catholic educators must determine as honestly and as accurately as possible what the needs of that people are, and then fill those needs as best they can.

Until this is done, one hardly need predict that resources now in short supply will continue to be squandered. Once a priority of need has been determined, however, it will be possible to use the same resources in a rational manner and with maximum effectiveness. Unless this is done—and done soon—there is danger that the educational effort of the Church will finally lapse into irrelevance.

Consider a typical parish. The parochial school, staffed largely by sisters but with a growing number of professional lay educators, enrolls about half the Catholic children of elementary-school age. Of the other half, a certain number (quite possibly a minority) attend CCD classes conducted by willing but largely untrained lay people. There is little or no contact between the school and the Confraternity. The parish's educational program is rounded out by an adult discussion club, the brainchild of a junior curate, involving perhaps a hundred couples. Like the parish school and the CCD program, adult education operates in isolation, neither influencing nor influenced by the other educational programs of the parish.

Nor is there any effort to mesh the educational efforts of different parishes within the same diocese. In education, as in many other programs under Church auspices, each parish operates largely on its own. It raises its own money, sets its own priorities, hires its own teachers, runs its own school. On the elementary level, its school offers a complete program from the first through the eighth grade. Its CCD unit is autonomous. Little or nothing is done by way of co-operation with neighboring parishes. The possibility that several parishes might share money, personnel and facilities —as by having the first four grades in one parish school and a "middle" school of grades five through eight in another— lies unexplored, even though doing so might save resources and at the same time make for better education.

Increasingly, however, the word "consolidation" is being heard among Catholic educators, and imaginative programs along these lines are being undertaken. It is too early to make a final assessment of consolidation in all places where it has been tried, but some of the results to date are decidedly encouraging. A nationally noted consolidation program carried out in the archdiocese of Dubuque, Iowa, has so far been a substantial success. Under the program, forty-nine smaller schools have been consolidated into eighteen larger administrative units, each with two or more attendance centers. Although the consolidation coincided with a 12 per cent decline in the number of teaching religious available to the archdiocese, it was able to make room for all but 8 per cent of the pupils previously accommodated in Catholic schools.

Mere numbers tell only part of the story. According to observers, the Dubuque experiment had such desirable academic results as eliminating double-grade classrooms; encouraging departmentalization; fostering the growth of middle schools; lowering the teacher-pupil ratio; promoting small-group and individualized instruction; and making staff specialization more feasible. The successful experience of interparochial cooperation has also given a boost to morale. As one observer of the Dubuque experiment has written, "Things heretofore thought impossible of accomplishment have been carried out with unbelievable rapport. It seems unlikely that any authority could have commanded the proposals that the people themselves created, adopted and supported."

Unfortunately, Dubuque is still an exception, and the pattern of isolated effort is all too common. The same pattern is often repeated at the diocesan level, where the chancery office may house a superintendent of schools, a diocesan CCD director, and a diocesan Newman director. However cordial their personal relations may be, their professional activities are carried on separately. There is likely to be no attempt to establish diocesan priorities in education, allocate funds and teachers according to those priorities, or otherwise coordinate their efforts.

On the national level the same pattern recurs. National Catholic organizations engaged in work related to education exist in large numbers, but there has been little contact among them. They have worked separately, met separately, and developed separate programs (some of which duplicate and overlap one another). They are more likely to have had working relationships with their counterparts in public education or other churches than with their Catholic colleagues.

This pattern—of autonomous, isolated fiefs and baronies in Catholic education—is the product not of perfidy but of history. The tragedy now is that an arrangement that has outlived its usefulness should be allowed to persist and to undermine the entire educational program of the Church.

To a great extent, the source of the problem is in the long-standing commitment to having every American Catholic child in a Catholic school. This was the mandate of the Third Plenary Council of Baltimore, which over the years has come in practice to mean identifying Catholic education with Catholic schools. The educational program of the Church was geared to the school; other educational ventures took place in a gray half-world, and were looked upon with indifference or outright suspicion. Parents who did not send their children to Catholic schools were regarded as at best marginal Catholics, and the educational services provided to their offspring were correspondingly marginal.

When the goal of "every Catholic child in a Catholic school" still appeared realizable, there may conceivably (although even this is doubtful) have been some justification for such an arrangement. Today, when Catholic schools on all levels enroll less than half the Catholic school-age population, and when there is every indication that this percentage will soon have declined still further, it is manifestly indefensible. A program that is locked into regarding Catholic schools as the only possible medium of Catholic education not only fails to deal with present-day realities but in effect condemns those whom it should serve to increasing neglect.

No one, of course, can say with certainty what the Catholic educational system of the future will look like. There seem, however, to be three principal alternatives. One is that the movement to "phase out" schools or grades will accelerate, to produce a situation in which a relatively small Catholic school system will be left to serve a relatively small minority (either the very affluent or the very poor—which group is, at this time, by no means clear). In that event, one may expect out-of-school religious education and religious formation programs to grow dramatically, in size and in scope.

The second possibility is that the Catholic school system will remain at about its present dimensions, neither expanding nor contracting substantially. Should this occur, Catholic schools will probably enroll a progressively smaller proportion of Catholic children of school age, since the total number of such children will presumably continue to grow while the schools are, numerically speaking, standing still.

Finally, it is at least possible that by heroic struggle and sacrifice the Catholic school system will be able to go on enrolling the same proportion of Catholic children of school age as now, or even perhaps to increase that proportion somewhat. Honesty, however, compels the admission that whether or not this is the most desirable alternative, it is at the moment the least likely of the three. Furthermore, even should it be realized, there will still remain millions of Catholic children and young people—to say nothing of adults—who, though potential clients of Catholic education, will never attend a Catholic school.

Some people may say that there remains a fourth alternative: a realization of the goal of "every Catholic child in a Catholic school," or of something close to it. Frankly, it is next to impossible to see how this could happen. The problem of money alone would seem to rule it out. Education is already a fantastically expensive business and becomes more so every day. Despite the growing affluence of the American Catholic community, its financial resources do have limits —and there are signs that these limits are being approached. (As the New York archdiocese's Committee on Catholic Education put the matter in a report made public in June 1969, it seems "unrealistic" to suppose "that the widening gap between educational costs and Church revenues can be met by people living at subsistence level in an inflationary economy.") Barring a radical and at present rather improbable reorganization of American education, which would see the federal government providing massive across-the-board support, including construction costs and teachers' salaries, to church-related institutions at all levels, Catholic schools will never be able to accommodate all Catholic young people. Even if, by some miracle, they could, the miracle would still leave untouched the problem of how Catholic education is to meet its newly acknowledged responsibility to such groups as the non-Catholic poor, or to Catholic adults.

The purpose here is not to argue which alternative is best. But it should be noted that up to now this crucial issue has had far less reasoned and documented attention than it deserves. What must be recognized is that although the alternatives exist, and a choice must soon be made among them, at present there is in most places no adequate machinery for making the choice.

It is possible, of course, to shirk altogether the responsibility of coming to a decision. In some respects this seems to be just what Catholic education is doing. At times the future of Catholic education appears to have been left to the operation of blind determinism. A school closes here, grades are dropped there, a CCD program totters on the brink of collapse in still another place, and no one does much about it. Voices are heard now and then prophesying doom, but such prophecies are usually issued in connection with a plea for the government to step in with a blank check, whereupon all difficulties will disappear as if by magic.

This is not meant as a criticism of those who argue for government aid to church-related schools. It is meant, rather, as a reproach to the Catholic community in general —and to the Catholic educational community in particular —for apparently preferring to let events take their "inevitable" course, instead of guiding them according to rational criteria and a consensus about objectives. Those with a concern for Catholic education should be acting now to determine its future. The alternative is simply to let things happen, with all the dangers such a course involves.

The choice among the several alternatives for the future of Catholic education should not, of course, be made arbitrarily or *a priori*. There must be a balance between the ideal and the reality—that is, between clearly defined principles and long-range objectives on the one hand, and on the other a very specific, hard-headed understanding of what is in fact possible, given the available resources. There must, furthermore, be the machinery for setting obejctives and priorities and for evaluating and assigning resources. Just how that machinery might function is a subject that must be spelled out in some detail.

Making Policy

What is needed is a policy-making machinery to represent all those who are affected in any way by Catholic education. Many views ought to be heard, and many areas of special competence drawn upon. This will require far closer integration among Catholic educational programs than at present exists, and far more communication between Catholic educators and the total community—Catholic and non-Catholic—than at present takes place.

To those who notice such things, important trends in this direction are already evident. On the diocesan level, for example, the office of "vicar for education," "secretary for education" (or whatever else the title may be) is becoming more and more common. This means that in a growing number of places the responsibility for coordinating educational work throughout the diocese is being assigned to a single office—in contrast to the old system, in which responsibility was parceled out among a number of totally uncoordinated individuals and offices. (There is, however, the danger in this development of an unhealthy tendency toward imposing coordination from above, instead of encouraging the responsible agencies, institutions and groups to work more closely together. Without dwelling on this point, it should be said that one-man rule would be no more desirable in Catholic education than anywhere else. In fact, precisely this sort of autocracy has been one of the problems of Catholic education. One should add the caution that a change in the organizational chart not be mistaken for the achievement of genuinely organic cooperation.)

Significant, too, is the growth of the board of education movement on the parish and diocesan levels. By 1969 there

were at least 4,500 such Catholic boards in the country, and
their numbers are still rising.

We shall have more to say about the implications of the
board movement in the following chapters. Here we wish
only to remark that lay boards may well point the way in
which Catholic education should move. They are unlikely
to be a transitory phenomenon. Indeed, it is possible that in
the perspective of history they will be seen as typical of the
most constructive changes in post-conciliar Catholicism, including the development of more democratic ways of making decisions that affect all members of the community that
is the Church.

Perhaps the most important thing about the board movement is the emphasis that these bodies should be boards of
education rather than *school* boards. Their responsibility is
to set policy—to establish goals and priorities—for *all* educational programs within a given parish, area or diocese, not
just for the schools. In a report appropriately entitled *Voice
of the Community,* a committee of the School Superintendents Department of the National Catholic Educational Association has urged that "the diocesan board of education be a
true board of education and not merely a school board.
Within the scope of its responsibility," the report goes on,
"should fall all formal educational activities of the Church
within the diocese. . . . Definitely included under the authority of the board should be all catechetical instructions,
adult education and the educational aspects of the Newman
apostolate. This concept of a diocesan board of education is
essential to the unification of the educational effort within a
diocese."

Concerning the rationale for boards of education, Father
Olin Murdick, superintendent of education in the Diocese
of Saginaw, Michigan, has remarked: "Education, as such,
is society's biggest business and concern. Catholic education,
which is no exception, can no longer be merely nor even

primarily an extension of the pastoral office. Questions on educational goals, programs and support involve decisions much too difficult and far-reaching for one person. Such difficult decisions demand an adequate decision-making process, one which involves both competence and consensus."

Logically, what is true at the parish and diocesan levels should also hold true at the national level. Coordination and cooperation among national agencies responsible for Catholic educational programs are equally essential. At the same time, however, one should not look for the establishment of a sort of national Catholic board of education that would set policy for all educational programs throughout the country. This would be entirely too centralized and monolithic an undertaking. American education has traditionally stressed the importance of keeping control of educational policy at the local level rather than vesting it, as is done in many other countries, in a central ministry of education. Theoretical considerations involving the democratic process, and practical considerations involving the management of educational programs in a nation as large as this, both argue that the traditional approach is the right one. And it is as appropriate for American Catholic education as it is for American public education.

At the same time, while rejecting the idea of a national Catholic ministry of education or anything of the sort, one can easily see the advantages, and indeed the necessity, of a much greater degree of collaboration among Catholic educational groups on the national level.

Such cooperation, for example, is essential to planning and even to conducting large-scale professional research of the kind that Catholic education badly needs. Considering the assurance with which positions are taken, commitments made, funds spent or withheld, the degree of ignorance concerning Catholic education is nothing short of astounding. The talk about dropping particular grades or levels from

Catholic schools in the interests of economy is a case in point. For all the vehemence with which this idea is both supported and attacked, there is little concrete information on what its educational results have been. To be sure, some rather convincing arguments against grade-dropping have emerged (such as that dropping the early grades appears to discourage children from enrolling in the upper grades and dropping the upper grades to discourage children from enrolling in a Catholic secondary school); nevertheless, even if ways could be found for coping with the practical difficulties, little is yet known about the crucial question of whether nonattendance at a Catholic school in, say, the first two elementary grades materially reduces the overall impact of Catholic schooling on a particular child.

Research, however, is only one area in which cooperation among Catholic educational agencies at the national level is needed. Still more pressing, we believe, is the need for intensive discussion of the broad goals, as well as the problems, of Catholic education. Recognizing the need for such dialogue, the National Catholic Educational Association in November 1967 sponsored a five-day Washington Symposium on Catholic Education. It was attended by more than a hundred people representing a wide range of views and disciplines—bishops, school superintendents, officials of the Newman apostolate and CCD, college presidents, leaders in adult education, teachers, journalists, government officials, businessmen and others. This was the first time so many capable people from so many fields had come together for serious talk about American Catholic education. It stirred up great interest and not a little opposition beforehand, the latter coming from those who feared either that the symposium would somehow legislate for Catholic education (a manifest impossibility) or that their own point of view would not be adequately represented (as may occasionally have been true, but was probably inevitable for a pioneering effort like this one). Within its own frame of reference, and despite the misgivings, the symposium went off well. It demonstrated the possibility and the usefulness of conversation among people with widely varying ideas about Catholic education, although it by no means settled the crucial issues that all of these people confront at present. It is essential now that such symposiums continue to be held.

It is also urgent that a permanent national organization embody the philosophy and the method of the symposium. One of the many useful suggestions to emerge from the symposium called for a national commission representing the various Catholic education-oriented agencies—NCEA, the Department of Education of the U. S. Catholic Conference, the Conferences of Major Superiors, adult education and so on. The commission would provide a permanent structure for cooperation among all these groups. It might also serve as a sort of national research council, empowered to treat problems calling for study, and to seek funds for the purpose.

Many unforeseen advantages would no doubt flow from the effort toward developing a unified program for Catholic education. Several major benefits, however, may be assumed in advance. A unified educational program would make possible the allocation of resources (money, teachers, buildings, and so on) on a rational and equitable basis. Some Catholic educators believe that at present there is an imbalance of resources expended on the students in Catholic schools as against those in public institutions, to say nothing of Catholic adults and the non-Catholic disadvantaged. It is certainly true that CCD and Newman have frequently been shunned as poor relations and obliged to make do with scraps from the table. Even if it should be found that the imbalance is only illusory, and that there are compelling reasons why the lion's share of available resources should go to the schools (and indeed we shall argue along these lines—

but with some significant modifications—in a later chapter), this can no longer be taken for granted. In any event, the policy decisions thus implied cannot be imposed arbitrarily from above without the assent of those affected by them; consensus within the Catholic community is necessary for any policy to be workable today.

Supposing, however, that an imbalance in the allocation of resources does exist, the solution is not, as some have suggested, simply to close down the Catholic schools, thereby abandoning their students to the same plight as the relatively underprivileged clients of the Confraternity and Newman. A unified educational program would, on the contrary, make possible for the first time a single responsible body equipped to appraise the situation and to decide how the available resources could be most effectively used. The alternative, it appears, will be continued acrimony over alleged discrimination, together with increasing intramural competition and a mounting waste of funds and manpower.

Such a program would also go a long way toward remedying the current crisis of confidence so troubling to Catholic educators. One of the basic causes of this failure of morale is the feeling, shared by many teachers and administrators (especially religious), that their best efforts and energies are being frittered away on an inefficient and relatively narrow form of apostolate. This feeling is reflected in the rush to inner-city work, picket lines and other activities where the need is believed to be greater and the emotional rewards more immediate than in parochial education. Unifying the church's educational programs would help to reinstill in these people the confidence (without which they will eventually either leave Catholic education or, remaining, become mere time-servers) that their services are truly being used in the best and most effective way.

Strong efforts toward unification would also help to relieve some of the current financial pressure on Catholic educational institutions. Federally funded programs, for instance, make it mandatory that Catholic educators within a particular community or state plan jointly and make joint presentations to government officials. It is quite certain that as they grow in sophistication, the Catholic laity—the traditional source of funds for Catholic education—will become less and less amenable to the idea of giving money to a handful of uncoordinated educational endeavors that show no sign of trying to eliminate duplication and increase efficiency.

It will, of course, be objected that pleas for the unification of Catholic educational programs are impractical because they run head on into frozen patterns of noncooperation and disunity. Any plan that would involve the pooling of personnel, for instance, touches immediately on the sensitive question of how to bring members of different religious communities together in the same institution or program. Yet if ever there was an artificial problem, it is this one. Surely no religious community can suppose that its *raison d'etre* will be destroyed if its members are obliged to work side by side with other religious. Religious communities that set their autonomy above the welfare of the Church are guilty of a strange reversal of values. Given the will, religious can certainly find ways of working together. Indeed, they have already done so: high schools and colleges in many parts of the country draw their faculties from several religious communities; and the Sister Formation movement and its schools have illustrated the possibility of close cooperation. Such cooperative patterns, however, now need to be broadened and placed on a firmer organizational basis.

What has been said of the religious communities is true of other organizational units in the field of Catholic education. The Church can simply no longer afford the luxury of parishes that will not cooperate with each other, dioceses that will not plan with each other, organizations that will not work with other organizations. The resources are too limited and the problems are too big to permit the continuation of such ecclesiastical *laissez-faire*.

3 Whose Schools Are They?

IF THERE is one problem which the Catholic school system apparently does *not* have, it is difficulty in knowing what its problems are. Nobody familiar with Catholic schools has trouble compiling a list of their problems, and although the importance assigned to individual items may vary, the lists themselves will almost always look much the same. They will, for example, surely include finances, the growing shortage of teaching sisters, the apparent difficulties many Catholic educators have in articulating a convincing rationale for Catholic schools, the issue of "priorities" (the inner city versus the suburbs), the challenge of providing excellent academic instruction, and the turmoil in catechetics. A reasonable man might well conclude that these problems are enough for any one school system. It hardly seems necessary to go looking for more.

Yet it becomes apparent in probing beneath the surface of the Catholic school crisis that another, fundamental problem takes precedence over most and perhaps all of the others. It is seldom discussed openly—in part, perhaps, because it is seldom clearly recognized, and also because it is (or seems at first sight to be) almost too difficult to be discussed. But it is hard to avoid the conclusion that most of the other questions now confronting the Catholic schools cannot be answered unless this one is. It is, quite simply, this: who controls—and who should control—the Catholic schools? Whose schools are they?

Many American Catholics would be tempted to consider this question either facetious or fatuous. The control structure of the Catholic school system has been so much a part of American Catholic life over the past century that it seems for many people immutable, not to say eternal. If pressed, most Catholics would say that Catholic schools belong either to the bishop within each diocese or to the religious orders that operate them. It is assumed that the schools serve the Catholic community (and, increasingly, the general community) but they do not in any real sense belong to the community.

This is a perfectly accurate statement. Catholic schools, with only a handful of exceptions, do belong either to bishops or to religious congregations, in the sense that ultimate decision-making power is vested in the bishops or the congregations. The real question, however, is not whether this is so (it is), but whether it should be so. Nor is the effort to find an answer an exercise in mere utopianism. For the conclusion is inescapable that the current state of affairs cannot long continue without damaging practical consequences.

This needs to be stated clearly. A radical rethinking of the control structure of Catholic schools is a pressing need for the American Catholic Church. The present approach seems, subtly but steadily, to be draining away support and vitality from the Catholic school system. Catholic schools are bleeding to death because they are locked into patterns of control that become less viable with every passing year. Unless action is taken, and taken soon, to place genuine control of the Catholic schools in the hands of the Catholic community (and even of the broader civic community, to the extent that it is served by the Catholic schools), the Catholic school system itself will be seriously endangered.

As with so many other problems Catholics now face, this one is the product of history—but not of very ancient history. Over the past century, the control of Catholic schools was vested in the hierarchy and the religious communities because no other arrangement was really possible. Given the inferior socio-economic status of Catholic immigrants and their children, the thought of allowing them a voice simply did not occur to those who had assumed the burden of establishing, owning and operating a massive school system. If there were to be Catholic schools, they had to be provided *for* rather than *by* the entire Catholic community. Alternatives were not so much unavailable as unthinkable. In retrospect this looks like paternalism, but at the time, being unavoidable, it was simply taken for granted.

The question of whether such paternalism is appropriate today may be put as two questions. First, is paternalism now a good idea? Second, will it now work? To both, the answer has to be No.

Paternalism in the control structure of Catholic schools is not now a good idea because is is being repudiated within the Catholic Church. One need not endorse a "one man--one vote" form of democracy in the choice of bishops or popular referendums on the acceptability of papal encyclicals to acknowledge that administrative procedures have changed and are continuing to change in the Church in response both to theoretical considerations and to popular desires. The ecclesiologists have scarcely completed their work in this area, but the vision of the Church enunciated at Vatican II has had profound reverberations both in the psyches of individual Catholics and in the day-to-day procedures of Catholic institutions. It is not possible to be definitive here, since Catholic thought on this point is clearly still in evolution. Certainly authority is not going to vanish in the Church, and Catholics continue to believe that Christ conferred ultimate authority in the Church on Peter and the Apostles—and on their successors, the pope and the bishops—rather than dispersing it equally among all members of the Christian community. But it is equally clear that the concept

of the Church as a community—as the People of God—
implies far wider delegation of authority and far greater
reliance on consultative and participatory decision-making in
practical matters than are customary at present. Surely Catholic schools ought to be as responsive as any other segment of
the institutional Church to what the concept implies.

Paternalism in the control structure of the Catholic
schools also will not work—or at least can hardly go
on working for much longer. Decision-making procedures
acceptable to a Church of immigrants a century ago are not
acceptable to a membership that is now predominantly middle-class and increasingly college-educated. People accustomed to having control of their own affairs in other areas
of life are not likely to acquiesce in unilateral decisions by
an authority—whether bishop, pastor or religious superior
—when it concerns the Catholic school. Continued one-man
(or one-woman) rule can only lead to widespread disaffection among the best educated, most prosperous and most articulate members of the Catholic community. Indeed, the
current malaise suggests that such disaffection is already a
reality for a large number of American Catholics, even
though they may not themselves yet recognize it for what
it is. The latent anti-clericalism which John Courtney Mur-
ray saw as a cloud on the horizon of American Catholicism
some years ago is still present, and can no longer be ignored
by Catholic educators. Many laymen seem to have lost confidence in Catholic schools, or to be on the verge of doing so,
because they perceive, quite correctly, that these schools are
not *theirs* in any real sense but are, rather, extensions of the
authority (and even the personality) of a clerical or religious decision-maker. They find themselves being asked to
support Catholic schools financially and, even more important, to enroll their children in them, without having anything to say on how these schools are run. The wonder is
not that many lay Catholics are less than ardently commit-

ted to Catholic schools, but that so many remain loyal despite the psychological roadblocks they find in their way.

Involvement of the Catholic community in the Catholic educational enterprise is now all the more urgent because of the radical changes occurring in Catholic education. Catholics have a right to express their views about its future and to play an active role in helping shape that future. Church leadership has an obligation to seek out the views of the Catholic community and to take these views into consideration.

If this is to be done, it will be necessary to find out what people really think about Catholic education. Happily, an effort to do so is becoming increasingly common in dioceses throughout the country. A professional survey of attitudes was, for example, an integral part of "Alternatives in Catholic Education," a joint study and action program developed for the archdioceses of Indianapolis and Louisville and the diocese of Evansville. The results have given educational planners in the three dioceses a clear picture of what Catholics think and feel about Catholic education.

The study made clear, for instance, that despite all the criticism of recent years, there is still a demand for Catholic schools. Eight out of the ten of the lay respondents to the survey agreed that "however hard it is to define, Catholic schools have a unique and desirable quality that is not found in public schools", and that every Catholic child should have at least some exposure to the former. At the same time, the survey indicated substantial division within the Catholic community over whether Catholic elementary and secondary schools should continue in their present form or be drastically changed. Lay people in general and pastors were split rather evenly, with about equal numbers for and against drastic change, whereas curates, sisters, suburban Catholics and so-called "Catholics at the crossroads" (parents whose school-age children were now in Catholic schools but who planned to send their pre-school children to public schools) were generally in favor of drastic reorganization.

One of the most controversial questions asked during the survey was whether, supposing a cutback in Catholic schooling were necessary, the elementary schools or the secondary schools should be closed first. Here the answers reflected a sharp division. Lay people expressed a clear preference for closing the high schools first (with 44 per cent in favor, as against 29 per cent who favored closing the elementary schools first); pastors were split rather evenly (37 per cent favored closing high schools first, and 34 per cent closing elementary schools first); assistant pastors favored keeping the high schools (56 per cent said elementary schools should be closed first, and only 22 per cent that high schools should be); and sisters voted overwhelmingly for keeping the high schools (only 6 per cent said they should be the first to close, whereas 74 per cent said the grade schools should close first).

Obviously, attitudinal surveys cannot by themselves set educational policy. They do, however, provide data that should play an important role in policy-making. Furthermore, they serve as a useful first step toward involving the total Catholic community in the process of thinking and planning for the future of Catholic education. At the very least, they give people a chance to be heard, an opportunity too seldom granted in the past. Such surveys also have an educational value in that they require people who perhaps have not been accustomed to think seriously and at length about Catholic education to weigh concrete alternatives.

But here, once again, an opinion survey is still only a first step. It is necessary to go beyond the mere eliciting of opinions, and to offer people the means for setting policy. One of the most encouraging developments in recent years has been the rapid growth, both in numbers and in competence, of Catholic boards of education as instruments for expressing the will of the community. The potential significance of the more than 4,500 parish and diocesan boards throughout the country demands that we look more closely at them.

Boards Of Education

Let the spiritual shepherds recognize and promote the dignity as well as the responsibility of the laity in the Church. Let them willingly employ their prudent advice. Let them confidently assign duties to them in the service of the Church, allowing them freedom and room for action.

In our parish we recently had an issue which caused a great deal of concern on the part of many individuals having children in the parish school. Attempts to get to the heart of the matter were met with a veil of mystery, just as in the past attempts to discuss matters of concern have been greeted with an attitude of hostility. The attitude has for some time been that, if we are not satisfied, we can transfer our children.

The first of these passages comes from the Second Vatican Council's *Constitution on the Church*. The second is from a letter written by a Catholic housewife and mother to her diocesan newspaper. Together they are a vivid demonstration of the gap between the ideal of lay involvement in the work of the Church officially espoused by the Council, and the reality—not simply of noninvolvement but of exclusion—that still prevails in far too many places.

This exclusion is particularly galling to laymen when it occurs, as it so often does, in regard to Catholic education. The Church has repeatedly stressed that in the education of children the primary right belongs to parents. Although both church and state exercise certain prerogatives concerning education, parents have the fundamental responsibility. Even when they delegate authority to the school, they retain both their duties and their rights in regard to the education of their offspring.

All this sounds fine—in theory. The trouble is that in practice, all too often, the theoretical right has proved to be a nullity. The parental "right" has meant turning children over to the school and thereby relinquishing effective control over their formal education. (This happens in public education, too, as witness the violent controversy over "local control" of education that has lately rocked the public school system.)

The problem has been complicated for Catholics by a benevolent authoritarianism (Father and/or Sister knows best), and by a lack of effective channels through which parents and other laymen could make their voices heard. Public education, whatever its problems of communication, at any rate has long had elected school boards; there has been nothing comparable for Catholic schools. The diocesan boards of education mandated by the Council of Baltimore—which have existed more often on paper than in reality—have been exclusively clerical bodies, with no pretense of representing the community served by Catholic schools.

Over the past five years, however, the growth of the board movement in Catholic education has begun to change the situation. Whether it alone can bring change fast enough and radical enough to save the Catholic school system remains to be seen. But if the board movement does not save the schools, it is difficult to imagine what else will.

Where properly prepared boards have been given an opportunity, they have been responsible for improving the salaries and benefits offered to teachers (and thus attracting a better quality of instructor into the Catholic schools), for upgrading teacher qualifications, for lowering the pupil-teacher ratio, and for promoting and supporting the use of new teaching techniques and materials, as well as encouraging diocesan and parish studies of Catholic education and making use of their findings in planning for the future. Much, however, will depend on whether the boards are allowed to function as they should. A board that is treated simply as an errand boy—by a pastor, a principal or a superintendent—is likely to accomplish little or nothing, and the experience of futility can be expected to leave its members with a bad taste in the mouth.

It would be stretching a point to suggest that laymen everywhere are clamoring for school boards, or for any particular means of increasing their involvement in the control of Catholic education. True, when asked directly, most laymen would probably say they favor the board concept. In June 1965, for instance, a referendum on the question was conducted throughout the archdiocese of Vancouver, British Columbia. Ninety percent of those who voted endorsed boards. But such evidence does not necessarily mean that Catholics in general are actively pushing for boards or other forms of lay involvement. Andrew Greeley and Peter Rossi report in *The Education of Catholic Americans* that only 7 per cent of a group of *Commonweal* readers, sampled as a "lay elite," believed that increased parental participation in decision-making was needed in Catholic schools. Greeley and Rossi expressed no particular surprise at this finding. "Parents have more than enough things to keep them occupied and are not eager for new responsibilities," they commented. "They would be much more concerned about the quality of education in their schools than about whether they had much to say about what goes on in them."

Since Greeley and Rossi conducted their study (several years ago), it is likely that attitudes have shifted substantially on this and other matters. Nevertheless, the extent to which Catholic parents still remain indifferent about the control of Catholic education is itself evidence of an unhealthy situation. For one thing, it suggests an apathy that could prove disastrous for Catholic schools. The crisis now facing the schools concerns not simply the quality of their educational offering, but their very survival. The Catholic layman has been conditioned to believe that he need not concern himself very much with the schools because, for one thing, they are not really *his* schools and, for another, they will always be there whether he is concerned or not—even though the continued existence of Catholic schools, at least in anything like their present numbers, is now very much an open question. By now, indeed, it is not fanciful to suggest that the schools will not continue to exist without a dramatic upsurge of lay interest, involvement and support. Boards are an instrument, perhaps the best one, for ensuring this lay commitment.

The theoretical arguments for Catholic boards of education, already noted, are equally compelling: namely, the primary rights of parents in regard to the education of their children, and the recognition of the role of laymen in the Church as the People of God. The Fathers of Vatican II might have been thinking specifically of boards when in the *Constitution on the Church* they urged the creation of "organs" to provide a medium for expression and action by laymen who, because of "knowledge, competence or outstanding ability," are qualified to "express their opinion on those things that concern the good of the Church."

Expression of opinion, however, is a rather pallid way to describe what an effective board of education can and should do. A committee of school superintendents of the National Catholic Educational Association has recommended that boards be more than merely advisory bodies, and that they function instead—as many are now doing—at both the diocesan and the parish levels as truly jurisdictional policy-makers. This has a more decisive ring of practicality. Today's layman is less than enthusiastic about what is implied by an "advisory" board of education, in which his opinion is solicited but can easily be ignored. There is no reason to suppose that laymen want to be the dictators of Catholic education, but neither will they be satisfied with a fiction in which they are "consulted" but not listened to.

Admittedly, defining the role of a board of education is not a simple task. In education as in other fields, policy-making is separate from administration, which is the domain of the professionals—the superintendents, the principals and the teachers. But the distinction between policy-making and administration, though easily made in theory, is often difficult in practice; and the built-in psychological attitudes that condition the way priests, religious and laymen look at one another are not likely to make it easier. As Father Olin J. Murdick has remarked, the real problems in the operation of a Catholic board of education "are not canonical or educational, but rather sociological, psychological and human."

It is not hard to imagine the nature of these "sociological, psychological and human" difficulties. On the part of the laymen, they are likely to appear in the opposing extremes of bumptiousness and timidity. After years of assuming that all the really important decisions about Catholic education were the province of bishops, priests and nuns, a layman placed in the role of educational policy-maker tends to react either by continuing the old habit of deference or by throwing his weight around. For bishops and pastors and priests, sister-principals and sister-teachers, the problem is a corollary one. A pastor faced by questions from a board of suddenly decisive laymen understandably feels that his authority is being threatened. The nuns, for so long the guardians of Catholic education, may sense that their professional competence is being challenged. Much patience, tact, good humor and consideration for the feelings of others, along with readiness to work together for the well-being of the schools and their students, are essential on all sides.

But even these virtues, however essential, will not in themselves be enough to make the new system work. Along with the establishment of a board of education, with jurisdictional authority over Catholic education in a given parish or diocese, must go an actual shift in the locus of decision-making. This must be understood, and accepted, if the shift is to take place at all.

Under the traditional American arrangement, the superintendent and the principal become in fact employees of the board by which they have been hired. Their duty is to carry out policy as set by the board and to report back to the board on how it has been implemented. Among Catholic educators, to put this into effect is clearly a reversal of roles of the first magnitude—one that for many, indeed, may seem virually intolerable. For what it really means is that laymen (not "lay people" as distinct from priests and religious, but people who are not professional educators) are to become responsible for setting educational policy.

Many advocates of boards not only accept this cheerfully but are its unhesitating proponents. The last Monsignor O'Neil C. D'Amour, one of the pioneers for Catholic boards of education, frequently insisted that lay control of educational policy was the peculiar contribution of the public school system in America, and should be applied without modification to American Catholic education as well.

Other educators, however, have been less sure. Admitting the value of lay participation (and therefore of boards), they nevertheless believe that Catholic education should not be too hasty in taking public education as a model. Public school boards are not without their own problems; in particular, it is not merely a possibility but a fact that an unenlightened or capricious board can adopt and enforce policies detrimental to sound educational practice. If Catholic schools are to adopt the board system, some educators say, it would be wise to learn from the mistakes of public education and provide safeguards against them—for example, by giving the professional educators significant representation in policy-making.

This is a reasonable objection. Perhaps all that can be said at this moment in the history of American Catholic education is that trial and error will be needed if a viable pattern of authority and operation for Catholic boards is to be found. Those concerned with Catholic education should not rush to adopt any one system. Patterns of control have a way of ossifying rapidly; habits and routines quickly become set; vested interests are not long in taking root. Catholic educators need a clearer picture than they now have of the consequences of various board systems before they settle unanimously and finally for any one of them. It might be better if, at the present time, several forms and combinations of "lay" and "professional" control were tried in different parishes and dioceses on a frankly experimental basis. One of the problems of Catholic education, and indeed of the Catholic Church generally, has of course been that such experimentation does not come easily; church administrators, understandably enough, prefer permanent structures with guaranteed results. But the pains, controversies and mistakes that come with any experiment will have been a small price to pay if the outcome is an effective reordering of the Catholic education system. It may be added that the drawbacks of any experiment are less severe if it is recognized to be just that.

One extremely difficult problem that must be dealt with intelligently in working out a new structure for the control of Catholic education is the relation of the schools to ecclesiastical authority. Within each diocese the bishop is ultimately responsible for the teaching of Catholic doctrine.

But if policy-making and true control are one day to be vested in the total Catholic community, how is the bishop to exercise his authority—an authority which is, of course, also a responsibility?

Here, once again, quick answers and ready solutions are not available. The problem is, of course, probably more hypothetical than real: it is difficult to imagine a Catholic community laying down, through its board of education, policies for the teaching of religion that are radically at variance with those of their bishop. Nevertheless, eruptions have already occurred in a number of dioceses over such things as sex education and the new catechetics. To date, none of these has amounted to a confrontation between the community and the bishop; they have been, rather, between the community (or segments of it) and the educators. But they do reflect a sensitivity to issues, and a tendency to polarize, that is growing among Catholics, and that in many places has made a tinderbox of Catholic education. The need for clear guidelines is, in short, becoming urgent.

One proposal has been to give the bishop veto power over decisions by the diocesan board of education (and the parish boards as well). Naturally, if a veto power exists, no board or other agency can be said really to control educational policy; at most the board will be operating at the pleasure of the bishop, with the knowledge that its decisions can be modified or even reversed if he chooses. Many advocates of boards of education reject such a provision, arguing that it violates the democratic rationale of the boards. But so long as various arrangements are to be tried on an experimental basis, it seems sensible to try this one, too. If there are valid objections in fact as well as in theory, they will soon be evident, and the arrangement can be modified accordingly.

Another proposal has been to make a clear distinction in Catholic schools between religious teaching and the teaching of "secular" subjects. The bishop might be vested with responsibility for the former, the board (or boards) for the latter. Thus, one can envision the bishop or his representatives designing and approving curricula for religious education, establishing standards for catechetical instructors, and otherwise exercising close control over doctrinal matters; in others, the board would have the final say. (Supporters of the "permeation" theory of Catholic education—who believe that many subjects have religious content or overtones —will object to this easy dichotomy between "religious" and "secular" education; but, without debating the theory, it can be observed that since the distinction is constantly made in practice, it might well serve as the basis for a pragmatic solution to this difficult jurisdictional question.)

A third proposal would give the board control over all aspects of the school's education program, leaving to the bishop the essentially negative function of deciding whether religious education in a particular institution did or did not meet certain criteria laid down for "Catholic" schools. A school that did not meet those criteria would presumably continue to operate but would not be entitled, at least until it arrived at a meeting of minds with the bishop, to describe itself as "Catholic," and the Catholic community would be so informed. (Naturally, the criteria would have to be clearly agreed upon, and perhaps there would be some mechanism of appeal for schools that fell afoul of bishops. The difficulties of arriving at both would of course be formidable.)

Whatever happens, it must be emphasized that the intent is not to challenge or undermine the authority of the bishop but rather to clarify that authority and make its exercise more responsive to the needs of the time. A squabble about the control of Catholic education would not only be undignified; in the present crisis, it might well mark the beginning of the end for Catholic education as a whole.

Granted, the bishop is the chief teacher in religious matters within his diocese; this is both his right and his duty. But the role of chief teacher need not carry with it the subsidiary roles of chief builder, maintainer and administrator of Catholic schools. Although these are separate tasks, in many places they continue to be borne by the bishop because the Catholic community is unprepared to shoulder them. But the time will come when these tasks must to a great extent be taken over by the Catholic community itself, leaving the bishop free to concentrate on functions that pertain more specifically to his role as chief teacher in religious matters. Under such an arrangement, the bishop would of course still be concerned with supporting and maintaining Catholic schools; the responsibility, however, would not be solely his, but would be shared with a cooperating Catholic community. The function of leadership would still reside in the bishop, but his leadership would be exercised in a new style and through new structures allowing for broader participation.

The same should be true of religious congregations, which in many places own and operate schools more or less independently of both the bishop and the general Catholic community. Increasingly, religious congregations are coming to regard their involvement in the ownership and control of institutions as an encumbrance in carrying out their apostolate. Some communities have already begun to turn over their holdings to separately incorporated lay boards (a process that is rather far along in Catholic higher education), and more can be expected to do so in the future. Such developments need not signal either the end of Catholic schools or the withdrawal of religious communities from the Catholic school apostolate. They should rather be seen as a frank and encouraging recognition of maturity on the part of the general Catholic community, and as a way of relieving the religious congregations of tasks—fund-raising, construction

and the rest—that can probably be performed more effectively by others, and which are not intrinsic functions of the
religious life itself.

The idea of entrusting the control of Catholic education
to the Catholic community is admittedly still new to many,
and thus likely to cause some alarm. Many people, for instance, may be fearful of the mistakes they believe a "lay"
board of educational policy-makers will make. Yet those familiar with the Catholic boards in operation at present
agree that in many places they have been an effective force
for improvement. Furthermore, members of a representative
board who are not doing their job, or are doing it badly,
can be removed from office by the community—as the
clergy and religious in control of schools, cannot, no matter how many legitimate complaints there may be from the
Catholic community. One of the strongest arguments in
favor of boards of education is thus their answerability; if
their performance does not measure up, out they go.

Nor is there any substance to the fear that religious will
lose their place as teachers in Catholic schools if lay boards
become universal. Catholic boards of education are without exception looking for more, not fewer, religious to staff
their schools, both because they respect the competence and
dedication of the religious and because of the substantial
economic saving their presence makes possible.

And what of those boards that ride some educational or
political hobby-horse to the detriment of the educational
program? Admittedly the danger here is real—but no more
so than the danger that exists under the present system,
where a pastor, say, may have similar predilections but is
much more difficult to unhorse.

The changeover to the system described here will not
come overnight; but, to judge from present trends, it may
come faster than many people suppose. It is essential, therefore, that much thought and careful planning be given to

the issue now. There should be room for trial and error, for experiment, for different approaches suited to particular places and people. It is too soon to impose a single pattern of control on American Catholic education for the next hundred years.

But at the same time, it is too late to suppose that the present pattern can continue much longer without serious consequences. Catholic schools cannot survive without the support of the Catholic community; and a significant number out of that community are not likely to go on supporting Catholic schools unless they are given more control over them. Those who hope to "save" Catholic education without radically altering its control structure are pursuing a hopeless objective.

4 Financing Catholic Education

NOT all the problems of Catholic education would magically vanish if large additional sums of money became suddenly available. Money would have little or no effect, for example, on the current decline in religious vocations, nor would it do away with the question of goals and priorities, or of the entire rationale for Catholic education. But money would make it easier to live with these problems, besides helping to relieve the near desperation that now accompanies the search for solutions.

Even these problems, furthermore, have their economic aspects. For example, the decline in the number of religious available as teachers in Catholic schools, and the consequent increasing reliance on lay teachers (who now comprise some 40 per cent of the faculty in Catholic elementary and secondary schools) means that they must be prepared to spend more in order to attract and retain competent people. And lest it be supposed that the problem is due solely to the growing number of lay teachers, it should be noted that the sisters are now—quite rightly—demanding and receiving higher salaries than in the past. Some Catholic educators have even suggested that the sisters be paid the same salaries as lay teachers, and then be obliged to pay the rent for their convents, along with other living costs, out of this income. This may not be a desirable arrangement, and it is surely not going to be put into practice overnight; but it does suggest the complications that can be expected in the years immediately ahead.

The problem of a rationale for Catholic education, too, has its economic aspect. As long as serious theoretical debate about the value of Catholic schools continues, one very concrete effect is likely to be a decline in financial support by those who no longer regard the schools as essential—or even very important—to the mission of the Church. And of course this works in the other direction, too. If doubts about the worth of the schools tend to undermine financial support, problems in financing schools tend to feed doubts about their value. When anything becomes as expensive as Catholic education is today, the normal human reaction is to take a step back and ask whether in fact it is worth all the blood, sweat and tears—and all those dollars.

The point to be made here is that the financial problems of Catholic education are not going to be solved in isolation from its other problems, just as the other problems are not to be isolated from the question of money. The financial problems of Catholic education can be dealt with only in connection with such matters as the composition of the teaching force and the equitable treatment of teachers, the setting of goals and priorities, and the control and policy-making structure.

One of the more striking things about Catholic school finances is that basic facts are so hard to come by. Opinions are another matter. We are repeatedly told that lay teachers are, or are not, underpaid; that tuition costs in Catholic school are, or are not, too high; that religious teachers do, or do not, represent very substantial monetary savings to the Catholic community. But reliable current data such as would give an accurate national picture are becoming available only piecemeal, where they are available at all, and vary widely in both quantity and quality.

Of the several reasons that can be cited for this situation, none is at all comforting. One is the decentralized character of the Catholic school system, which in many places is hardly even a "system" but rather a loose grouping of isolated, semi-autonomous institutions. Another is the lingering supposition that Catholic school finances are somehow nobody's business—nobody's, that is, but the pastor's or the superior's, or whoever happens to keep watch over the books. The trouble with supposing it to be "nobody else's business" is that it risks being taken literally, and leads to suspicion or to mere indifference toward Catholic education. People especially resent being patronized by those who are simultaneously asking them to hand over their hard-earned money; and the Catholic school administrator who today pursues a policy of ironclad secrecy in money matters is likely to find himself sooner of later without either money or a school.

One thing known with some certainty about Catholic schools is that, despite all their failings and unsolved problems, they are relatively efficient in their handling of finances. An exhaustive study by Ernest Bartell, an economist at the University of Notre Dame, of school operations in two urban dioceses—one in the Midwest and one on the Pacific Coast—found that in thirty-eight of thirty-nine public school districts Catholic school costs averaged less than 60 per cent of public school costs. Since studies have constantly shown that Catholic school students do at least as well on standardized tests of academic achievement as their public school counterparts, it appears that these savings, which could be matched elsewhere in the country, are not achieved at the expense of quality. (Granted that standardized tests are not the ultimate measure of educational accomplishment, they do nevertheless provide at least a rough comparison between systems, and their testimony is consistently favorable to the Catholic system.) The savings in Catholic schools seem, rather, to be attributable to the dedi-

cation of Catholic educators, to frugality in the use of resources, to a willingness to cut corners on nonessential items
of plant and equipment, and to the absence of a large, centralized administrative bureaucracy. It would thus appear
that wider public disclosure of the facts about Catholic
school financing would uncover neither scandal nor extrava-
gance in money matters. The picture would, on the contrary, almost certainly be both edifying and instructive—yet
another reason for regretting the lack of data.

But despite evident thrift and relative efficiency in the use
of resources, Catholic education remains an expensive proposition, and is becoming more and more expensive. Bartell's
study of elementary schools in two dioceses found that between 1958 and 1964, operating costs per pupil rose nearly
50 per cent; and it is safe to suppose that costs have risen at
least as fast since then. Although they remain substantially
below the cost per pupil in public schools—for the reasons
mentioned above—the increase has nevertheless brought
about a genuine financial crisis in many parishes and
dioceses. At the secondary level, costs rose 13 per cent in one
of these dioceses and 16 per cent in the other over the same
period. (It is well to bear in mind that costs per pupil in secondary schools average from two to three times as much as
at the elementary level.) The fact is that costs per pupil in
Catholic schools in recent years have risen faster than
price levels in the economy as a whole. Teachers' salaries
are probably the largest single factor in this rise; moreover, they can only be expected to account for a larger part
of the budget as more and more lay people are added to the
Catholic school teaching force, and as they become more
militant in pressing their just demand for salaries comparable
to those paid to teachers in public schools.

Another way of looking at finances is to see how large a
slice of total parish and diocesan expenditures has gone to
Catholic education. Bartell found that in 1963 the parishes

of one diocese that maintained schools put about 60 per cent of their total expenditures into elementary education. These same parishes—60 per cent of all the parishes in the diocese —accounted for 85 per cent of parish expenditures. And, on the diocesan level, almost 50 per cent of the operating expenditures for all institutions and activities went into schools.

It is not often acknowledged, and still less often appreciated, that the schools have been enabled to survive up to now thanks in large degree to the contributed services of their teachers. Out of a sense of commitment, religious and lay teachers alike have worked for a fraction—often an astonishingly low fraction—of what was paid to their counterparts in public education. George Shuster, the distinguished Catholic educator now at the University of Notre Dame, says he came to understand the human meaning of "contributed services" when, seated one day at Mass near the sanctuary of the university chapel, he noticed that nearly all the sisters who knelt at the Communion rail wore half-soled shoes. Bartell, employing another yardstick, estimated the average value of services contributed by each of its religious teachers during the year 1963–64 at $5,425 in one diocese and $3,572 in another. The picture was the same on the high school level. Furthermore, the equivalent value of these contributed services has obviously risen substantially since Bartell's study, as teachers' salaries and benefits continue to increase rapidly. "Contributions" on the order of $3,000 to $5,000 or more annually per religious teacher are very substantial indeed. But how long can Catholic education reasonably count on this largesse? As noted, the ratio of religious teachers to lay teachers is declining, and lay teachers are more expensive, even though their decision to teach in Catholic schools generally means a substantial economic sacrifice. Furthermore, even the salaries paid to religious as teachers are rising and, as we have seen, it is being suggested in some quarters that religious be paid on a par with lay colleagues. No doubt Catholic education can expect for some time—perhaps even indefinitely—to benefit from the dedication of its teachers, but it cannot count on doing so to the same degree as in the past. Catholics simply cannot—nor, in equity, should they—expect to preserve their schools by underpaying their teachers. A trained and competent teacher today is an extremely valuable property, and if Catholic schools are to remain competitive in the quality of their offering, they must be prepared to bid for teachers on the open market with salaries very close to those available in public schools. Many schools, indeed, are already doing so.

Where will the money come from? There is no easy answer to that question. The traditional sources of support for Catholic education have up to now been adequate—if no more than barely so—to the job at hand; it is difficult to believe that they will continue to be adequate in the future. At present the principal sources for maintaining Catholic schools are tuition and fees, the contributed services of teachers, and donations. We have already seen the dimensions of the burden that dependence on contributed services imposes on the teachers. Tuition and fees, along with donations, place the burden on a particular group of Catholics who in the nature of things are least able to bear it. Uniform tuition and small donations are, it has been pointed out, essentially regressive in that they take proportionately a larger share from those with relatively low incomes than from those with relatively high incomes. It is obvious that for a family with an income of $8,000, Catholic school tuition costs of, say, $400 per year are a heavier burden as compared with the family whose income is $12,000 but for whom the tuition costs are the same. Similarly, revenue-raising by "pay-while-you-play" method—bazaars, breakfasts, dinners and so on—tends to place a heavier burden on the low-income family. The result, as Bartell says, has been that although education in America generally has been the "philanthropy of the rich," education in the American Catholic Church is in fact the "philanthropy of the poor."

Even within the traditional structure of ecclesiastical fund-raising by voluntary donations, remedies for this situation are possible. One proposal is for progressive tithing, under which the well-to-do would contribute a larger percentage of their income than would the less affluent. Certainly the burden of supporting Catholic education should be shared by the entire Catholic community—as is true of public education—and not merely by those who happen to have children in school at a particular time. Another possibility, little explored up to now, lies in securing endowments for Catholic elementary and secondary education. All voluntary methods of producing revenue are hampered, of course, by the same fundamental problem: they *are* voluntary and lack means of enforcement. Although this is an arrangement no one within the Church would wish to change, even if change were somehow possible, it points once again to the inescapable fact that Catholic education, if it is to survive, must involve and be supported by the Catholic community to an even greater degree than is true at present. Many observers are convinced that this can be done— that, given the facts about the financial problems of Catholic education, Catholics will respond. But the facts must be given, and the community, in responding, must be assured of having a voice in how the money is spent. Fortunately, the means for giving the community a voice now exist—namely, in Catholic boards of education, whose potential we have discussed earlier.

Beyond a doubt, the growing problem of financing Catholic education has meant a renewed interest in other than traditional sources of funds. One current proposal is to enlist the support of business and private industry. The appeal, it is suggested, should be less to the altruism of businessmen than to their sense of economic realities. Catholic schools represent a tremendous tax saving to business and industry—a saving that would disappear if the schools were forced out of existence for financial reasons, so that business and industry would be required to pay substantially more in taxes to support a public school system swollen by an influx of students formerly in Catholic schools. In view of this, businessmen might reasonably be asked to pass along some small percentage of their dollars-and-cents saving to the source of the advantage, namely to Catholic education.

To help Catholic educators make better use of what they already have, some observers have recommended a program to train Catholic school administrators in sophisticated techniques of planning and budgeting. Anthony Seidl of the University of San Francisco has gone so far as to assert that the need for money in Catholic education is in fact "less acute than the need for better ways to use it." His statement has made a number of people quite angry, and it may well be that he is overstating the case. But it also seems evident that defective planning and budgeting procedures (inherent in decentralization) and frequent reliance on untrained financial officers, are responsible for a number of problems among Catholic educators. Fortunately, the situation is improving. The combined pressures of government aid programs, diocesan and regional centralization, and the desire to do a more professional job, have led to better financial procedures in many places. And the National Catholic Educational Association, aided by a grant from the Ford Foundation, recently conducted a year-long program to train a corps of Catholic school people in up-to-date techniques for long-range planning.

For financial as well as educational reasons, much more thought, study and practical experiment with regard to new educational techniques are necessary. Among others, the possibility of "home learning centers" consisting of television, telephone and computer linkups, though it sounds far-fetched today, may be a reality tomorrow. If so, the future may find most children doing a substantial part of their "school" work at home, and coming to school only one or two days each week. In the school itself, will teaching machines and other devices reduce the number of teachers needed and make it possible to rely more on para-professionals? Or will technology in fact turn out to require more teaching manpower—in addition to huge initial investments in equipment? Most educational planning, Catholic and otherwise, is now being done on the basis of conditions and methods that may already be obsolescent, if not obsolete. This is bad for any school system; in the case of Catholic education, already hard pressed for funds, it becomes almost total folly.

It is also folly to cling to a parish structure which, so far as educational financing is concerned, has neither rhyme nor reason. Theorists may continue to argue among themselves as to whether or not the old-style geographical parish is "dead"; but whether it is or is not, the parish as an economic unit more and more simply does not make sense. The financing of Catholic education demands that funds (and personnel) be able to flow freely across parish boundaries. Central financing, professionally administered, is essential; so is central purchasing; so is long-range planning, regional and diocesan.

Public Aid

Any discussion of new sources of funds inevitably leads to the subject of federal (and other governmental) aid to education. At the federal level, American education in general and Catholic education in particular, appear to have reached something of a plateau—if one can reasonably describe the economic stringencies forced by the Vietnam war and the problems of an inflationary economy in this way. So long as military expenditures are continued at their present staggering height and the overheating of the economy remains a serious danger, no large new federal aid programs can be expected; the likelihood is a period of treading water, and even of reductions in existing programs. There is, however, a general expectation that once the Vietnam war is over, substantial new programs of aid to education will sooner or later be enacted by Congress. Figures of from $5 billion to $10 billion have been mentioned, and suggest the possible magnitude of the new thrust in federal aid. Clearly, it is time for educators to review the past and plan carefully for the future.

The pervasive theme and rationale of aid programs up to the present, as Shuster notes, has been the recognition of education as a valuable national resource, essential both to the solution of particular problems and to the maintenance of national well-being. In the G. I. Bill of Rights, for instance, institutions of higher education, public and otherwise, have served as instruments for demobilization. The National Defense Education Act gave aid to schools, nonpublic as well as public, for improved training in science and languages in response to what was seen as a national emergency after the Soviet Union's dramatic successes in space. The Elementary and Secondary Education Act of 1965 made funds available to improve the education of the poor. In doing so, the government quite reasonably acknowledged that poor children are still poor whether they attend public or nonpublic schools, and accordingly extended benefits to both. Almost certainly the next great thrust in federal aid will be based on the recognition that education is a precious national resource and should be treated accordingly. This being so, it is hard to see how Catholic schools could logically be excluded on the grounds of public policy, since they now enroll five million American children and young people a year.

In recent years nonpublic school educators have based much of their case for government assistance on the so-called "child benefit" theory. They have argued that, although it may be possible to debate the constitutionality of direct aid to church-related schools, aid to the students in these schools or to their parents must surely pass constitutional muster. In fact, aid administered in this way seems almost super-constitutional, since its effect is to broaden the options of students and parents in the choice of schools, and thus to put flesh on the otherwise rather skeletal right to freedom of choice in education.

In June 1968, the decision of the U. S. Supreme Court in the New York textbook case (*Board of Education v. Allen*) upheld a state law under which public funds are used to buy and lend books to students in church-related schools. As a result, the long-range prospects for achieving equitable treatment for nonpublic school pupils under government programs of aid to education were substantially improved. In the key passage of the majority opinion, Associate Justice White wrote as follows:

Underlying these cases [previous decisions involving government assistance to nonpublic education], and underlying also the legislative judgments that have preceded the court decisions, has been a recognition that private education has played and is playing a significant and valuable role in raising national levels of knowledge, competence, and experience. Americans care about the quality of the secular education available to their children. They have considered high quality education to be an indispensable ingredient for achieving the kind of nation, and the kind of citizenry, that they have desired to create. Considering this attitude, the continued willingness to rely on private school systems, including parochial systems, strongly suggests that a wide segment of informed opinion, legislative and otherwise, has found that those schools do an acceptable job of providing secular education to their students. This judgment is further evidence that parochial schools are performing, in addition to their sectarian function, the task of secular education.

This, it should be noted, represents a significant and probably realistic movement away from the "child benefit" theory. Mr. Justice White's argument is that nonpublic schools in fact perform a public service ("the task of secular education"), from which it follows that they can legitimately be aided from public funds for this segment of their educational program. Thus, rather than having to ride on the shoulders of their students ("child benefit"), nonpublic schools now have warrant from the Supreme Court to argue for governmental aid because of the contribution they make toward achieving the acknowledged objectives of American society. Within days after the Supreme Court's action, this principle was given concrete expression: the Pennsylvania state legislature enacted a "purchase of services" program giving financial assistance to nonpublic schools, including church-related ones, for the secular aspects of their educational program. Since then, nonpublic school educators in several other states have begun to press for similar legislation. At this writing, similar successes have been achieved in Connecticut, Rhode Island and Ohio.

Nevertheless, it would be foolish to imagine that all obstacles to governmental aid have been removed by these developments. On the contrary, major difficulties remain. At the state level these include legislative apathy or indifference, the continued opposition of traditional opponents of public assistance to nonpublic schools, and the highly restrictive provisions of a number of state constitutions concerning aid to church-related institutions. At the federal level, in addition to the present (but presumably temporary) reluctance to adopt large new federal spending programs, there is also the certainty of further litigation contesting present programs of federal aid to nonpublic schools as well as any that may be enacted in the future. Such litigation was in fact virtually invited by another ruling of the Supreme Court at the time of the Allen decision, which held for the first time that taxpayers do have "standing" to challenge federal spending programs on First Amendment grounds. Up to now, furthermore, the Supreme Court has held that nonpublic school *pupils* may share in tax-supported programs of aid to education; presumably there will be controversies over whether church-related *schools* may receive direct governmental assistance. This may, of course, be a distinction without a difference; but the question has yet to be resolved by the courts, and this will not happen overnight.

For these reasons, among others, it is unrealistic to look to government aid as a total and immediate solution to the problem of financing Catholic education. Certainly every challenge should be fought in the courts. Nor should the supporters of Catholic (and other nonpublic) schools be apologetic about doing so. The legislative process is after all meant to be used, and is being used, vigorously and continually, by individuals and groups in pressing what they believe to be their just claims.

To be sure, nonpublic school supporters should not be obnoxious or unduly disruptive in their efforts—as they would be, for example, if a threat to close parochial schools because of financial pressures were used to bludgeon lawmakers into providing funds to keep them open. But there is nothing wrong with pointing out that many parochial schools *will* have to close their doors if some public assistance is not forthcoming, or with drawing attention to the inevitable consequences—namely, crowded public schools and soaring tax rates—that could be expected. These things cannot be disputed, and it is both right and responsible to make sure that they are widely recognized.

All such efforts, however, will take time, and the financial crisis in Catholic education is already at hand. Even while they bend every effort to obtain government aid, Catholic educators will be making a tragic mistake if they count too heavily on it to bail them out of their difficulties.

One can expect the wrangle over the use of public funds for students in nonpublic schools to continue in Congress, in the state legislatures and in the courts for years to come, even though the position taken by doctrinaire advocates of the separation of church and state is not merely unreasonable but foolish.

If the separationists succeeded in their fondest dreams, and church-related schools were squeezed out of existence by financial pressures, American education as a whole would be crippled. The public schools already have their hands full in educating the students they now enroll and there are no visible signs that the public would agree to still higher taxes for the expansion of public education that would be necessary if the five million students in Catholic schools became the clients of government schools.

Of course, in some quarters the notion lingers that it would somehow be a good thing for the country if there were no church-related schools. But no one has ever demonstrated how this benefit would come about. On the contrary, common sense suggests that it is to the advantage of public education to have a strong partner in the nonpublic sector willing and able to shoulder part of the burden of educating the country's young people. The irony is that the right of nonpublic schools and their students to be full partners in the American educational enterprise should be under serious constitutional attack at precisely the moment when leading figures in education are urging that this partnership be closer and more complete than ever before.

Much of the new emphasis on partnership is related to the educational crisis in the cities. For example, at the National Catholic Educational Association's 1968 convention in San Francisco, the U. S. Commissioner of Education, Harold Howe II, called on Catholic schools to assume "a part of the burden in educating the urban poor." Some, including the writer and social critic Christopher Jencks, have suggested that the government contract with private groups to set up innovative educational projects in the inner cities. A similar plan—for the purchase by the government of the services of nonpublic schools—has received support from the other end of the ideological spectrum, namely a task force of the U. S. Chamber of Commerce.

Quite clearly, the crisis in American cities—educational and otherwise—is so vast that every agency with anything to contribute toward resolving it should be encouraged. Howe made plain his own belief that Catholic schools have much to contribute, chiefly because their organizational structure cuts across city boundaries, and because their relative freedom from political pressure and bureaucratic red tape would permit them to become vehicles for experimental programs in educating the disadvantaged. It would be disheartening to see Catholic schools denied the opportunity to respond fully to this national need because of a rigidly doctrinaire interpretation of the First Amendment.

Yet it would be unrealistic to suppose that once all constitutional and legislative hurdles have been cleared, Catholic schools need do no more than say in effect, "We're ready to help," and proceed to line up at the window where the money is handed out. If Catholic schools want to be full partners in American education, they will have to prove their readiness for partnership. They will have to play according to the rules of the game. These rules were made quite clear at the Washington Symposium on Catholic Education in November 1967, by Philip Des Marais, Deputy Assistant Secretary of Health, Education and Welfare. If Catholic schools are to participate significantly in federal aid programs, he said, several things will be expected of them. One is "complete disclosure of financial operations." It would be "inconceivable," Des Marais said, that "any federal funds could ever be made available directly to non-public schools . . . without the available data on the exact per-pupil cost of annual operation of the schools participating." Finally, Des Marais said, "I think a whole new complex of relationships involving information and contact between your schools and your congressmen with respect to the whole issue of what you are doing, what you are contributing in the way of educational services, how much it costs, what your problems are, is absolutely necessary if you are going to have any role in the future ball game." To this one might add that closer relationships are essential not only at the federal level but also with state and local governments, where many of the most important decisions are made about requesting and allocating federal funds. As one Catholic education official has put it, "We need eye-to-eye contact between public and nonpublic educators in thoroughly planning [ESEA] programs. We must learn to understand and appreciate one another's goals."

The message, then, is clear: there must be contact, communication, salesmanship. Adequate financing of Catholic education depends on an ability to convince the public that funds are not only needed but deserved, that Catholic schools today are making an enormous contribution to the well-being of American society, and that the country would be poorer without them. Above all, Catholic schools must be recognized as true "community" schools, serving not just the special interests of the Catholic Church but the social and educational interests of the nation. A school system that educates one out of every eight American children must regard itself, and be regarded, as an essential component in the pattern of American education. The sooner Catholic schools are viewed in this light, the nearer they will have come to a lasting solution of their financial problems.

Even a lasting solution, however, cannot be expected to guarantee the continuation of every Catholic school now in existence. No doubt some additional funds for Catholic education can be found within the Catholic community and in the private sector of the economy; beyond doubt, Catholic school administrators can be trained to make better use of their financial resources, and their efficiency can be improved by centralized financing procedures; and quite possibly increased state and federal funds for the "secular" and "public service" aspects of the Catholic school program will sooner or later be forthcoming. But none of these developments individually, and probably not all of them together, will be enough to cope with the rapidly worsening financial crisis in Catholic schools.

This does not mean that all or even most Catholic schools need disappear; but some (and perhaps many) inevitably will. Clear and specific decisions about the role to be played by the remainder therefore become far more urgent than in the years when the number of Catholic schools was still rising. It will be essential for Catholics to decide what their schools should accomplish, and then to see to it that the schools in fact do so. We will take up this crucial issue as we discuss goals in the chapter entitled "Schools for the Future."

The finances of Catholic schools are intimately bound up with the composition—and the treatment—of their school teaching force. Probably more than any other group, these teachers will determine the future of Catholic education. We shall then next turn our attention to them.

5   The Teachers

AMERICAN teachers are in a mood of radical and wide-ranging discontent. For the last several years, headlines have spoken of massive, noisy and sometimes violent protests, demonstrations and work stoppages by teachers. It is not that they have become advocates of violent revolution; teachers remain, on the whole, stable and even conservative. But they are also confused and angry, uncertain of the place they occupy in society but persuaded, correctly or not, that they have been consistently exploited by a public which wants quality education at bargain prices, and manipulated by bureaucrats and pressure groups anxious to protect their own special interests at the expense of teachers.

This is not the place for a full-scale examination of such problems and complaints. But no discussion of teachers in Catholic schools can pass over the fact that they share many of the complaints of American teachers generally. Of course, the Catholic school teaching force has some special, and grave, problems of its own. Perhaps the best way of elucidating these problems, both shared and unique, will be to examine three roles played by the Catholic school teacher. They may be summed up under three headings: the teacher as professional, as militant, and as apostle.

The Teacher as Professional

Teaching, we are told, is a profession. Even while accepting this as the view teachers usually hold of themselves, one may ask exactly what it means. To look upon teaching as a profession is in fact quite new. It is only in the last seventy or eighty years that any special preparation for those planning to become teachers has been thought necessary. Many people now alive can remember the time when it was generally assumed that any young man or woman with a high school education, or less, was capable of taking over a classroom in an elementary or even a secondary school. Such primitivism is naturally to blame for its share of educational disasters; yet similar disasters still occur today, in classrooms presided over by bright young persons equipped with degrees and teaching certificates. The "professionalization" of teaching is a good thing, to be sure, but it has been no panacea.

Thus it is not uncharitable, but merely realistic, to point to the element of snobbery that exists in teachers' insistence on their professionalism (as it does, of course, in other professional groups). Today many callings have become "professions" that formerly claimed no such status. It is not our intention to deny that people in such fields are professionals in a true sense. The complexity of contemporary knowledge and techniques, and the concomitant necessity for rigidly specialized preparation, have indeed produced many new "professions," of which teaching is only one. But at the same time it is evident that one reason for the insistence on their professionalism by these new professionals is their desire to set themselves apart, in their own eyes and others', from working people. (It is not so long, after all, since we stopped speaking of working people as "common.") The American dream is essentially a middle-class phenomenon, even if it now eschews lace curtains in favor of a suburban house with a barbecue grill on the patio. If there is one thing the *nouveau*-professionals of American society dread, it is dirt under their fingernails.

The ideal of professionalism is commendable. It can raise the aspirations and the performance of individuals and groups as a whole. But if teachers are to function as professionals, they must have a clearer understanding of what professionalism entails; and this understanding should begin with a stripping away of snobbery and pretension. In many ways the effort to elevate teaching to a profession has the mark of social and academic status-seeking. Professionalism in education has become a kind of race to keep up with the Joneses (i.e., the other, older professions) by building up an intricate superstructure, on which all the trappings—special degrees, graduate schools, professional societies too numerous to mention, professional journals too numerous to read, and an all but impenetrable jargon—have been strung out like the decorations on a Christmas tree.

As we hope is obvious, we are not attacking degrees in education, graduate schools, professional societies or educational journals. (Educational jargon—"educationese"—is another matter.) What we *do* challenge is the shoddy reason for which these things are sometimes sought and valued in the educational community: not as the means of enabling teachers to do a better job, but as status symbols that demand automatic deference from anyone not so endowed. The situation perhaps says more about the insecurity of the teachers' image of themselves than about the justice of their claim to be regarded as professionals.

To clarify the understanding of professionalism as applied to teaching is no easy task, especially since members of other aspiring professions seem equally unsure of their own status. There are, however, certain possible avenues toward clarification. One is a return to the old and often disparaged notion that the teacher should be competent in regard to *what* is taught before becoming excessively concerned with *how* to teach it. Emphasis on content over technique flies in the face of what has long been accepted by many educators. The old ideal never entirely disappeared from the scene, however, and it has an increasing number of advocates today. Knowledge and skill are both important, of course; but precisely because command of a subject and skill in teaching it cannot be separated. Overemphasis on teaching methods, however, can be at the expense of the subject matter, with ineffectual and indeed unprofessional teaching as the result.

Substantial obstacles now prevent the recognititon of this principle. In too many places the curricula of schools of education and the requirements for certification of teachers seem inextricably bound up with the insistence that method take precedence over matter. But in the years ahead, as the debate continues, it should become clear that to be truly professional, a teacher must first of all be in command of the subject to be taught, even if some courses in method have to be sacrificed as a result.

Another requisite, if teaching is to become truly professional, is that the noninstructional functions a single teacher is now commonly expected to take on be redistributed among a corps of personnel, relieving the "professional" teacher of all but the real task of teaching. Apart from low pay, perhaps the chief grievance of teachers today is the load of nonteaching chores they must assume. Taking attendance and collecting "milk money" require little training and have still less to do with teaching skill; but, as any teacher so burdened can testify, they use up an inordinate amount of time and energy. Contrast with the medical profession makes the anomaly apparent. It would seem a bit odd to find a surgeon presiding at the registration desk in a hospital lobby, serving meals to the patients, or toting up bills at the cashier's window, with an occasional exercise of skill in the operating room; yet this is analogous to what the classroom teacher is customarily called upon to do.

One solution to the problem that is much discussed today calls for the use of teacher helpers—non-professional or subprofessional aides who would assume the noninstructional

chores of classroom administration. Of the elaborate plans
that have been developed, one would divide the current
"multipurpose" teaching role among five distinct categories
of personnel: teacher aide (supervising lunch and recess,
clerical work, and so forth); teacher assistant (preparation
of teaching materials, marking assignments, helping with
instruction); teacher associate (in effect a beginning
teacher); certified teacher (the fully qualified professional instructor); and supervising teacher (overseeing the work of
the rest). Some critics regard such a reorganization of teaching functions as both impractical (largely because of cost)
and excessively rigid. Perhaps no one plan will be ideal. Yet
it is obvious that as long as teachers are required—as they
now are—to perform an excessive number of nonteaching
tasks, their morale will continue to be low, the dropout rate
for teachers will be high, and the definition of "professional" teachers will remain unclear.

An interesting proposal, made in June 1969 by a special
study group, the Committee on Education for the archdiocese of New York, suggested the establishment of a
Catholic Teacher Corps. In the words of the proposal, it
"would consist of volunteers who would work for the subsistence stipend rather than for secular salary: young graduates and graduate students of universities, married women
whose income is not required for the support of a family—
persons who wish to engage in service to their fellow man
even at personal sacrifice." Obviously, to be effective, the
members of such a corps could not be simply of well-inten-
tioned but unqualified persons willing to work for low
wages. The New York committee, evidently recognizing
this danger, added that it should be "mandatory that all
such persons be appropriately qualified for the work undertaken." Given this essential condition, however, such a corps
could be a valuable response to the need for both teachers
and paraprofessionals in Catholic schools.

Everything that has been said about professionalism applies as much to Catholic school teachers as to those in public schools. The issue takes on an added dimension, however, in the context of Catholic education—namely, the question of whether lay people and religious stand on the same footing and, if so, how this is put in practice in the assignment of teaching and administrative jobs.

In 1967 the Washington Symposium on Catholic Education took a stand that has had increasing support: "Professional competence should be a primary criterion in filling teaching and administrative positions in every area of Catholic education. Professionally qualified lay men and women, clergy and religious should be equally eligible for every type of teaching or administrative positions." On its face this would seem to be a flat endorsement of the principle of hiring "the best man for the job." And so it very nearly is—but not quite. For it may be noted that the statement speaks of professional competence as *a* primary criterion for filling positions, not *the* primary criterion. It also specifies that laymen, clergy and religious should be equally eligible for every *type* of position; this is not necessarily the same as to specify every individual job. Although this may appear to be hair-splitting, the qualifications may in fact be justified under present circumstances. Abstract pronouncements are easily made, but less easy to apply in a particular situation. What is important now is that the idea of merit assignment, and promotion on the basis of merit, be accepted in principle in Catholic schools, and put into effect so far as is feasible; and this is what is happening now in an increasing number of places. Whether the principle can be applied in every situation is a matter to be dealt with according to the facts of the case and on the basis of common sense.

The remarkable thing is that this principle should still seem at all radical. The habit of reserving certain jobs in Catholic schools for priests or religious is so firmly entrenched even now, in some quarters, that to question its relevance—not to say prudence—is to be guilty of audacity. The cause, of course, lies in the history of American Catholic schools, which for decades have depended for their very existence on the willingness and availability of priests and nuns (especially the nuns!) to staff them. There was no one else to do the job, and the clergy and religious assumed the burden in a spirit of courageous generosity. Although this generosity can be measured in economic terms—the smallness of the stipends traditionally paid to teaching sisters—money tells only part of the story. Behind those stipends is the human sacrifice involved: round-the-clock devotion during the school year, an unrelenting pressure to amass credits during the summer session. This kind of devotion, year after year, was plodding and unglamorous, and for that reason all the more impressive.

Devotion, however, can go only so far in making up for a deficiency in numbers, and that deficiency has meant a radical change in the composition of the teaching force in Catholic schools. Throughout the phenomenal expansion of the Catholic school system in the 1940's and 1950's, the number of priests and religious also continued to rise, although nowhere nearly as fast as the number of schools. That lay teachers had to be hired to staff these burgeoning institutions was a matter not of principle but of necessity. Thus in the school year 1957–58 out of a full-time teaching force in all U. S. Catholic schools totaling 147,330, there were 35,129 lay teachers; whereas for 1967–68, the number of lay teachers had risen to 90,066, out of a teaching force of 206,959.

All present indicators suggest that the proportion of laymen in Catholic education will continue to rise for the foreseeable future. It is true that the era of the massive expansion of the Catholic school system is past. But another factor now seems to guarantee a growing numerical preponderance of laymen: the decline in priestly and religious vocations. However one may explain and deplore the vocations crisis, it is a fact of life. Perhaps the current trend will be reversed in the near future; perhaps not. In any case Catholic education must live with present realities, not past achievements or future hopes. The reality now is that religious habits and Roman collars are gradually disappearing from the Catholic school classroom, even though they will certainly never vanish altogether. If it is to survive, the Catholic school now must look increasingly to lay people as teachers and administrators.

Since this is so, the Catholic school has to offer lay people adequate reasons for committing themselves to a career in Catholic education. The opportunity for apostolic service and the expectation of financial reward are two such reasons; they will be examined below. But in addition, Catholic schools should also give lay teachers and administrators the opportunity to advance as far and as fast as their ability permits. Careers in Catholic education need to be made professionally attractive to laymen. The applicants' state in life can no longer be the deciding factor in assignment and advancement. To insist that it be so is to entrust Catholic education to the ministrations of persons of undoubted zeal but dubious competence, or worse still, to apathetic hangers-on for whom self-improvement and professionalism have little importance. It goes without saying that this is not a description of the lay teachers and administrators now serving in Catholic schools. But as professionalism becomes a hallmark of American education generally, Catholic education will find increasing difficulty both in retaining the competent lay staff it already has and in attracting new laymen of outstanding ability unless it allows lay people to achieve professional advancement.

The trend toward full opportunity for professional growth by lay people in Catholic education is already evident. In Catholic colleges there have been lay professors and chairmen of departments for years, and now laymen as deans and presidents are becoming increasingly numerous. The breakthrough achieved in higher education is now being repeated at the elementary and secondary levels and in diocesan school offices. A partial survey in 1968 disclosed that there were lay superintendents of schools in two dioceses, as well as a total of thirty-eight lay principals of Catholic elementary and secondary schools. These numbers, though small, take on significance as one reflects that this state of affairs would have been unthinkable as recently as five years before, and that it is the beginning of a movement toward full professional participation by laymen in Catholic education.

Objections are sometimes raised to this, as they are to any major development. Some are real, some fanciful; in this time of transition, all deserve notice. Among them are the following:

1 Some religious communities still think of Catholic schools as "ours" (meaning theirs). This is less an objection than it is a statement of fact. Although it is understandable, since Catholic elementary and secondary education has been almost the exclusive responsibility of the religious communities for decades, it seems destined to disappear as newer developments come to be recognized. One is the change in the control structure of Catholic education that is now in process. As more and more lay boards of education take their place as policy-making bodies, it will become clear that the schools do not "belong" to any one segment of the Catholic community but rather to the community as a whole. As this realization sinks in, religious communities will be less inclined to think of the schools as theirs. The process will also be speeded by the rise in the number of lay teachers and administrators, which is inevitable because of the decline in religious vocations. Once the proportion of lay teachers in Catholic schools throughout the nation passes 50 per cent

(as it soon will), religious and clergy will no longer find it possible to think of the schools as "ours" in an exclusive sense; "ours" will of necessity include laymen on an equal footing with priests, brothers and sisters.

2 Some clergy and religious find it unsettling and perhaps even psychologically impossible to conceive of having to carry out their duties under the direction of a lay administrator. For that matter, some lay people may likewise feel ill at ease and perhaps incapable of functioning in a supervisory capacity over priests, sisters and brothers. In all likelihood, however, this will prove to have been passing phenomenon. Once the shock of novelty has worn off, laymen, clergy and religious should find no particular difficulty in working together as professionals. The proof of this is that it is already happening in a number of dioceses and schools. In some cases the transition may be uncomfortable, but the necessary psychological adjustments can and will be made.

3 It has been suggested that priests and religious may find themselves in the schizophrenic dilemma of having to serve two masters, one a religious superior and the other a lay administrator. More and more often, however, the two jobs of religious superior and institutional administrator are now already assigned to separate individuals, both of whom are either clergy or religious. Where the two are compatible, those who work under them have no particular problems; where they are at odds, the situation may very well be awkward. But there is little reason to suppose that the awkwardness will be worse if the administrator happens to be a lay person. The question in other words, is not one of laity versus clergy and religious, but rather of good working relations between human beings. There is no intrinsic reason why these relations should be either better or worse simply because an administrator is a layman.

4 Emphasizing the layman's role in Catholic education and giving him professional status equal to that of the priest

or religious, including access to the more highly paid administrative jobs, will mean increased costs for Catholic schools—and, in all likelihood, the death of more than a few institutions forced out of business by financial pressures. It would be pointless to deny the probability of such an event. We believe there is no way to deal with this problem except through the measures outlined in our chapter on financing: that is, through better planning and budgeting procedures, and through centralization of diocesan school finances, along with improved methods of raising funds in the Catholic community and in business and industry, and through obtaining increased tax support. Even so, it seems doubtful whether any or all of these measures will be sufficient or come soon enough to save all the Catholic schools now in operation. How large a number will be forced out of business for financial reasons, no one can say; but the increased role of laymen as teachers and administrators will have been a contributing factor.

Yet what alternative is there? Even now, as we have seen, there are not enough priests and religious to go around; and there will be still fewer in the years ahead. Catholic schools, if they are to survive, will simply have to find competent laymen to staff them. To do so, they will have to offer salaries that are competitive—or which, if they do not equal, at least approximate those paid in public schools. For the school that pays substandard salaries will in most cases today have to settle for substandard personnel; and an influx of over-age or undertrained laymen into Catholic school classrooms and administrators' offices would cause the schools to lose the support of many sophisticated Catholic parents in short order.

Some things can be done now to prepare, financially and in other ways, for the inevitable changeover to a school system staffed heavily by laymen. One proposal is to do away with the traditional subsidy by the parish to the sisters who teach in its schools (free convent quarters, free food, free

car, and so forth) and instead offer the sisters a flat—and equitable—salary, plus benefits, out of which they would pay
their own living expenses. Sister Mary Luke Tobin, Superior General of the Sisters of Loretto, has argued that by
shifting to such an arrangement now, schools and parishes
can avoid the abrupt and traumatic shock of later having to
find the money for laymen to replace sisters leaving because
of death, illness, defection or the decline in vocations. A
phased movement toward compensation of sisters at something approaching their fair market value might, by antici-
pating a future crisis, help to forestall it.

In a more general way, Catholic schools ought also to
give serious thought to the matter of "product differentia-
tion." In other words, Catholic schools need to demonstrate
that they provide an education significantly and desirably
different from that available in public schools. Up to now it
has perhaps been too easy to assume that the "difference"
lay largely if not exclusively in the fact that most teachers in
Catholic schools were priests or religious. But if more and
more Catholic school teachers in the years ahead are going
to be laymen, the schools will have to show that their educational program is distinctive for reasons other than their
teachers' state of life or clothing. We shall offer some
suggestions as to where this difference lies in our chapter on
the reasons for Catholic schools; here, however, we merely
note the problem as one intimately related to the fact that
laymen inevitably will assume a larger role in Catholic education, and that professional competence, rather than state
of life, will become increasingly relevant in deciding who
gets which job in the Catholic school of the future.

The Teacher as Militant

The militancy of teachers is an escapable fact of life in
current American education. Although the biggest and nois-

iest explosions so far have occurred among public-school teachers, strikes and controversies have become rather common in Catholic education as well. It would be a delusion to suppose that this trend will diminish: as a matter of realism one can only assume that it will grow.

What accounts for the militancy of the teachers? Many factors are responsible. One is that men now make up more than 50 per cent of the teaching force in public secondary schools, and their numbers are still rising. Male teachers, it is reasoned, are naturally more combative than women. Furthermore, most of them have families to support and need salaries that are correspondingly higher.

Teachers' salaries, although they have risen rapidly in recent years, still lag behind those in most other professions (and even those of many skilled workers). A strike in February 1968, by public school teachers in Montgomery County, Maryland (a "bedroom" suburb of Washington, D. C.) won them a minimum starting salary of $6,340, and a maximum of $12,870 for an experienced teacher with a master's degree. But at that time the average household income in affluent Montgomery County was $13,653.

The demand of teachers for a "voice" is another part of the picture. Teachers resent creeping anonymity and the feeling that they are no more than cogs in a bureaucratic machine. Obviously, too, they are unhappy at finding themselves pawns in what they see as an economic and political game of chess. This helps to explain the determined stand by the 55,000-member United Federation of Teachers in New York during the bitter conflict over decentralization and neighborhood control of the city's public school system.

Finally, it may be said, teachers have learned a lesson from the militancy of old-line labor unions, civil rights organizations and even dissident students. Demonstrations and other forms of aggressive behavior have paid off in results for these groups on many occasions, and teachers have concluded that they are entitled to make use of similar tactics.

Rivalry among teachers' groups has added more fuel to the fire. The two big contestants are the American Federation of Teachers, a branch of the AFL-CIO, and the National Education Association. Each has its own state and local affiliates. The AFT, with about 140,000 members, has made militancy its keynote and has leveled charges of "company-unionism" at the NEA, whose 1.1 million members include administrators as well as teachers. By its victories, AFT has succeeded in what might never have come about through words alone—namely, in moving the giant NEA toward a more militant posture. Now that the union has won the right to represent teachers in New York, Baltimore, Washington and other cities, the NEA has begun to shift from its traditional reliance on quiet pressure and, in rare cases, "sanctions," toward a tougher and more activist stance. Whereas NEA's former Executive Director, Dr. William G. Carr, was an outspoken opponent of teacher strikes, his successor, Dr. Sam M. Lambert, has said, "We will not encourage strikes, but if one occurs after all good faith efforts fail, we will not walk out on our local groups." The implications of this statement became apparent in February 1968, when the NEA and its Florida affiliate, the Florida Education Association, supported the first statewide teachers' strike in the nation's history.

It is by no means clear how the contest between the union and the association will turn out. Within the NEA, angry administrators have threatened to withdraw from the association completely if it continues to support teacher strikes. Despite efforts at a compromise, this must still be counted a possibility. Some observers predict an eventual *rapprochement* between the union and the association; and in fact David Selden, the AFT's national president, made a merger one of the chief goals of his administration. Although the association up to now has rejected any such proposal, it has been suggested that in many parts of the country the merger may become a *de facto* reality at the local level as teachers look for the most effective organization for pressing their demands.

None of this can allow Catholic educators to be complacent. Militancy among teachers in Catholic schools is a few years behind militancy among public school teachers, but the trend is there, and has already been manifested by Catholic teachers in several large dioceses. In Catholic schools the problems connected with teacher organization and collective bargaining are, furthermore, even more complicated than in public schools. Whatever period of grace Catholic educators may be privileged to enjoy must be used wisely to anticipate the day—perhaps not too far in the future—when militancy and all its hallmarks are as common among teachers in Catholic schools as they now are outside them.

Salaries are probably the biggest single reason why at least the lay teachers in Catholic schools now look favorably upon organization and collective bargaining. Although the figures are now badly out of date, it is worth recalling that in 1962–63, according to the Notre Dame study of Catholic education, the median salaries for lay teachers in Catholic elementary schools were $3,145 for women and $3,555 for men; at the secondary level the median was $4,010 for women and $4,803 for men. Despite everything that can be said in mitigation—that the schools could not afford more, that those who teach in Catholic schools are willing to make sacrifices, that most of the teachers, or the women anyway, probably do not rely on their salaries as their sole means of support—the fact remains that these figures are appallingly low. Matters have improved greatly since 1962–63; in a number of dioceses and schools, salary scales have been set at from 90 to 95 per cent of those in public schools. But many teachers in Catholic schools are still paid substantially less than their public-school counterparts.

Catholic educators simply cannot any longer afford a policy that pays their teachers markedly less than the public schools do. Unless marked progress is made, one of two things will happen: the schools will be forced into the desperate (and ultimately deadly) expedient of hiring unqualified people willing to accept inadequate salaries; or else lay teachers, by demonstrations, strikes and other displays of militancy, will force school or diocesan officials to accede to their demands.

Since many Catholic schools sooner or later are going to have to deal with some form of collective bargaining, they should begin now to plan for the day, by developing procedures that will direct militancy toward constructive channels rather than into angry protest. E. Riley Casey, general counsel of the National School Boards Association, at a meeting in 1968 of the Division of Elementary and Secondary Education of the U. S. Catholic Conference, called for the drafting of a model employee-relations code for Catholic schools. Without attempting to spell out the details, Casey pointed to eight areas of "primary concern" that such a code might cover: a guarantee of the right of employees to organize; a guarantee that such an organization would be the sole bargaining agent for the employees; the recognition by employers of an obligation to bargain with such an agent; the recognition of strikes and other "impasse procedures"; provision for determining the appropriate bargaining unit, with specific regard to the question of whether supervisory personnel should be part of it; a guarantee to employees of freedom from coercion either by an employer or by an employees' union; a guarantee of stability in the bargaining relationship (barring "raids" by one union on another's territory and providing that the status of the employee organization would not be challenged during the life of a contract); and provisions for enforcement, either through arbitration or by setting up a permanent board of inquiry.

Catholic educators also need to give close attention to the form that future collective bargaining is likely to take. A choice may one day have to be made between the two approaches to teacher organizations that are represented by the union and the association (the same choice, it should be noted, need not be made everywhere). Decisions will also have to be reached about the complicated question of relations which clergy and religious faculty should have to the teachers' organization.

The question of whether to form a union or an association is one of the most controversial for American educators today. From many points of view, belonging to an association would usually appear to be preferable, since an association generally has broader goals and interests than a union, which in practice tends to limit its concern to economic demands. Furthermore, whereas the union admits only teachers, the association is open to supervisors and administrators as well, thus making it possible for all educators to work together instead of being polarized into warring camps. On the other hand, there is a danger that the association may turn out to be a "company union," controlled by administrators and unresponsive to the needs and desires of teachers. Nevertheless, in the climate of today's educational scene, it can reasonably be argued that this is less of a danger than the threat of polarization represented by the union.

The association, with its emphasis on "professional" concerns, also may offer a more viable means of bringing together laymen and religious in the same organization. For at least as long as religious teachers remain economically on a different footing from lay teachers, it is difficult to see how, even as members of a union, they could share very many economic concerns with their lay colleagues. And there are practical reasons for asking what could be the function of religious in a teachers' union, since typically they are far more concerned with improved professional status than with salaries and benefits. Ideally at least, the same question would not apply to an association with purposes and objectives that went beyond purely economic matters.

Nevertheless, that the association may be preferable in theory to the union does not mean that it will necessarily be so in practice. In some places Catholic teachers have no alternative to militant unionism in pressing their demands for fair salaries and benefits. Where this is so, lay teachers may even have to exclude religious from becoming members, if their doing so appears likely to undermine the legitimate purposes of the union. (Some Catholic teachers' unions have already taken this position—whether fairly or unfairly, the authors are not prepared to say.) Perhaps all that can be said now on this complex question is that teachers do have a right to organize; ideally, they should choose a form of organization whose goals are not exclusively economic, and which encourages cooperation among all educational personnel instead of dividing them into hostile camps; but where efforts have been made in good faith, and have failed, Catholic school lay teachers must be accorded the right to go it alone, using union organization and union tactics to press for fair treatment.

Faced with such a situation, Catholic school administrators, especially priests and religious, make a serious error if they respond automatically with rigid hostility and with strikebreaking tactics. This has already been the reaction in some Catholic schools, where "outside" priests, brothers and nuns have been brought in to handle the classrooms during a strike by lay teachers. Certainly, administrators have a duty to place the students' interests first, and they will naturally seek to keep the schools functioning even under great difficulty (particularly when they judge that the students' chances for, say, college admission may depend to a large extent on their doing so). At the same time, however, they should take a careful look at the long-run possibility that by injecting a residue of ill will among lay teachers, such tactics may do permanent damage to the quality of the school program. The best advice (more easily given, of course, than acted upon) is that everything possible must be done to avoid the angry confrontations that lead to strikes and all their disagreeable consequences.

At the moment, the question of teacher organization is wide open among Catholic educators. It will not remain so for very long. The pressures toward militancy and toward organization in the ranks of public school teachers are growing among Catholic school teachers as well. If plans are not made now for responding to the teacher as militant, Catholic schools will soon find themselves forced to respond in a setting of crisis.

The Teacher as Apostle

The Catholic school teacher today must find a way of balancing and reconciling the three roles that education, society and the Church have assigned to him—his role as professional, as militant and as apostle. Ideally there ought to be no strains or conflicts in fulfilling the three roles, but life unfortunately is not that simple. The teacher may find that his professionalism and his militancy lock horns in a practical situation, and that no theoretical formulation can possibly do justice to its complexities. Nor is it possible to introduce, with a flouirsh, the concept of apostolate—like a rabbit drawn from a hat—and resolve the teacher's inner conflicts by elevating them to a higher synthesis. Ideally, perhaps, it may do so. Practically, however, the notion of the apostolate only adds another dimension of complexity to any understanding of the task of the Catholic teacher today. For "apostolate" has itself become one of those catch-all concepts that, under the strain to which all Catholicism is now subjected, are so burdened with obsolete practice and half-formulated aspiration as to be on the point of collapse.

In order to arrive at a concept of the teaching apostolate that has meaning today, one must begin by getting rid of certain notions which, although commonly associated with the idea, in reality have no direct connection with it and may in fact be harmful. One of these is the exaggerated emphasis on self-sacrifice (one might even speak of the "mystique" of self-sacrifice) that appears to surround any discussion of the role of the Catholic teacher. In many quarters it is still assumed that a teacher in a Catholic school should be prepared to make not merely the usual sacrifice of time and of physical and emotional energy any good teacher expects to make, and which can in fact be immensely rewarding—but others that by any reasonable standard exceed the call of duty.

Thus, as we have seen, the lay teacher in a Catholic school has frequently been expected to work for wages and benefits drastically below those available to his counterpart in the public school. Even more galling, perhaps, is that he has been obliged to renounce most forms of accepted professional recognition in a system where the positions of greatest prestige and authority as often as not have been reserved for priests and religious. As for the religious teacher, he (or more often she) has been called on not merely to sacrifice certain physical amenities, but also to take on staggering work loads, and to accept assignments that are frequently uncongenial as well as debilitating. Nuns in particular have been obliged to devote themselves to school-related tasks from early morning until late at night, seven days a week. Even their summer vacations are likely to have been spent in a seemingly interminable struggle to acquire credits toward an advanced degree. Since religious are generally trained to accept whatever job is assigned to them, often there has been little attention to personal inclination or even fitness for the assignment. Thus men and women unsuited for the task have found themselves serving as administrators; born administrators have been assigned to the classroom; teachers who might have done a commendable job at the high school level have had to cope with elementary classes and vice versa.

There is no need to exaggerate the situation. Not all Catholic school teachers have been exploited financially, repressed professionally, or assigned to jobs for which they are unqualified. On the contrary, many have found great personal and professional rewards in education. But too many have been overworked, underpaid and subjected to extreme frustration—all in the name of a "sacrifice" thought to be intrinsic to the teaching apostolate.

Considered pragmatically, however, the practice has been self-defeating. It has not furthered the apostolate but has undermined it. The mark of the apostolate should not be that it is agonizing but rather that it is effective. To demand impossible sacrifices is not to increase but to diminish its success by destroying those who carry on the apostolate. Integral to the mission of Catholic teaching must be the objective of enabling teachers to use their own skills as effectively as possible. Whatever hinders them in this— whether it be low pay, excessive work loads, uncongenial assignments or lack of opportunity for professional advancement—is a disservice not only to the individual teacher but to the apostolate itself. The exaggerated mystique of self-sacrifice must now be consigned to the ecclesiastical dustbin. A concept of apostolate built around the *de facto* exploitation of teachers cannot be justified either theologically or pragmatically.

But if the idea of self-sacrifice can no longer be required as the foundation of the teaching apostolate, what is to take its place? The answer would seem to lie in the idea of witness. The teaching apostolate must be a witness to the relevance of Christ and Christianity to all that is embraced by the concept of education: the search for truth; the encouragement of personal growth—physical, intellectual, moral and spiritual; the application of knowledge in the service of human life and as a testimony to the Creator of whom it is a reflection. By what he is and what he does, the Catholic teacher is a witness to all of these things. The better the teacher, the better the witness will be. And whether religious or lay, a Catholic teacher bears witness to the compatibility of his own state of life with the goals of education, and, in turn, to the compatibility of the Christian faith with the goals of education as a whole. There is not only room, but a need, for both religious and lay teachers in the apostolate of teaching. That the Catholic school offers a setting for the fullest possible witness of this kind is a compelling argument for its existence. It is not, however, an argument for herding those who are unable or disinclined to teach—whether they are religious or laymen—into classrooms simply in order to keep the "system" going. A grudging or incompetent teacher makes a poor witness and does harm to the apostolate. This is not to say that every Catholic school instructor must be a superlative teacher (that would be asking the impossible). But an effective apostolate requires that every teacher enjoy what he is doing, want to do it, and be at least reasonably skillful at it.

The challenge of redefining the apostolate is particularly urgent for religious teachers. Religious communities themselves are in a state of ferment and confusion. Powerful surges toward renewal and change, given impetus by Vatican II, are sweeping through religious life today. Yet in many respects the "renewal" has not fulfilled the confident expectations of only a few years ago. The number of new vocations to the religious life has declined steeply; the number of those leaving the religious life has increased. In the long perspective of history all this may be seen as a transitory phenomenon, the prelude to a rebirth; but at the moment it is a source of confusion and alarm. It is beyond the scope of this book to analyze or pass judgment on what is happening in religious life, but some comments are in order.

One fact of overwhelming importance is that today's "new breed" of religious is a very different creature from his or her predecessors. Automatic obedience and docility are now in question, and in many instances have been rejected; personal self-fulfillment is regarded as essential. In many respects this is the inevitable—if largely unanticipated—consequence of the drive by Catholic educators toward self-improvement over the past twenty years. There has been a significant effort, largely through the Sister Formation movement, to upgrade the professional and personal training of women in religious orders. A growing number of sisters have emerged from behind the convent walls and onto college campuses, to mingle on terms of academic equality with students and professors with very different backgrounds and attitudes. As a result, today's woman religious has personal and professional qualifications largely unknown in sisters of previous generations. But it cannot be ignored that the emergence of the "new nun" has destroyed forever the traditional source of an unquestioning and always available work force for Catholic schools.

Not everything about today's "restless religious" (as one author calls them) is commendable. There is a point beyond which a legitimate concern for personal satisfaction and fulfillment becomes ordinary selfishness. It seems as if some contemporary religious were bent on having the best of both worlds: the freedom of the layman to choose his own work and social life, and the freedom from economic worries and personal insecurity enjoyed by the "old breed" of religious. This is certainly a comfortable arrangement, but one wonders how much connection it has with the genuine apostolate of religious life. Some of today's newly "liberated" religious also manifest an adolescent spirit in their rejection of authority and their uncritical enthusiasm for the latest fad, intellectual or religious. Adolescent enthusiasm has its merits, but it lends itself to the dangers of disillusionment when the novelty has worn off. It seems possible that the disillusionment observable in some religious today is of this adolescent sort: scornful of the old, disenchanted with the new, they have come to the unreasonable conclusion that somebody or something has let them down.

Be that as it may, the implication is nevertheless clear that the religious teacher today must be treated equitably and as an individual. Some sisters, with a good deal of justice, liken their situation in the Church (and that means, for most nuns, as Catholic educators) to that of the Negro in American society. As the black man has been the "invisible man" in America, so the sister has been the "invisible woman" in the Catholic Church: exploited, neglected, patronized and not infrequently bullied. All this must be changed. Indeed, it is safe to predict that if all else fails the sisters themselves will change it—not so much by rebelling as by simply vanishing. The drastic dropoff in the number of new candidates entering many women's religious communities, and the increasing number of those leaving religious life, are warnings that Church leaders, including those in education, must not ignore.

A number of practical steps ought to be taken immediately. Personnel practices in the Church must be radically overhauled. So far as is humanly possible, religious must be assigned to positions for which they are suited by taste, ability and training; the old "who's-available-now?" system of handing out assignments must be abandoned once and for all. Religious must be consulted about the jobs they are to fill, and their preferences given every possible consideration. Many communities have begun to do this; in the future, all of them must. Consideration should also be given to the proposal that religious be allowed to contract individually for jobs. There are many obvious practical difficulties in the scheme, and it may never be universally workable. Yet it deserves at best to be treated as a serious and responsible suggestion.

Some will see in such proposals the imminent demise of Catholic schools. Indeed, giving autonomy to religious in their choice of a career does mean that whether or not they will serve in the schools is now up to *them*. But once again the basic question must be faced: what is the alternative? Religious are already disappearing from Catholic schools; to try to hold them there by force may only hasten their departure. If there are religious teachers in the Catholic school of the future, they will be there because they have chosen to be. Indeed, if there are to be any teachers at all in Catholic schools, it will only be because of their free, personal choice. The apostolate of Catholic education must now be prepared to prove its value and importance to the teachers themselves. Catholic school teachers—professional, militant and apostolic—are waiting for that proof. They will not wait forever.

6   Why Catholic Schools?

THIS whole book has been written out of the conviction that, in the present realities of American society and the Catholic Church, Catholic schools are neither a self-indulgence nor even a pleasant luxury, but are in fact indispensable, both to society and to the Church. We realize that this is a strong statement, but it is not made casually; and we shall now try to explain and defend it.

Up to now we have spoken of ways to strengthen and continue Catholic schools. But prescriptions for improving them are irrelevant if those schools should not or need not exist. Enormous effort now goes into maintaining the American Catholic school system, and even more enormous effort will be required to maintain it in the future. It is therefore obvious that either there must be excellent—indeed, overriding—reasons for the continued existence of Catholic schools or they should be closed down as rapidly as possible, with due allowance for Catholic sensibilities and for the capability of the public schools to absorb their students.

It goes without saying that other uses could be found for the money and the personnel now devoted to Catholic schools. Yet it would be simplistic to assume that the resources now given over to the support of Catholic schools would or could be more or less automatically diverted to other apostolic purposes. Most of the current financial support of Catholic schools comes ultimately from the Catholic laity, and it may be questioned whether they would be willing to contribute as heavily to other church-related or church-supported undertakings as they have to the schools.

(It may be that they should have been educated to do so—although, as will be seen below, we believe their commitment to the schools, even in preference to other institutions and programs, has been reasonable and even praiseworthy.) Furthermore, since most of the staff in Catholic schools, both religious and lay, are teachers by vocation and training it is doubtful that many could be shifted to other vocations. This is not in itself, of course, a sufficient argument for retaining Catholic schools; but as a cautionary matter, the feasibility of reallocating all of the financial and human resources now devoted to the schools is not to be ignored.

It remains true, on the other hand, that the support of Catholic schools now places a vast burden on the Catholic community. If that burden could be lifted, many people would breathe a sigh of relief. One direct way of removing the burden would be to dispense with the schools. And in view of this the question must be faced realistically, are Catholic schools necessary?

It should be borne in mind that the answer was not a foregone conclusion even in the nineteenth century, when the commitment to a massive Catholic school system was made by the American Church. At the time, despite widespread dissatisfaction in the Catholic community with the Protestant orientation of the public schools, at least some Catholic leaders argued for exploring the possibility of a cooperative effort, designed to mesh Catholic religious instruction as closely as possible with the public system of education. With the advantage of hindsight one can say of such an arrangement that, had it worked, it might perhaps have been nearly ideal. Efforts in this direction were made during the later years of the nineteenth century, notably in Poughkeepsie, New York, and in the Minnesota towns of Faribault and Stillwater. Existing Catholic schools in largely Catholic areas were leased to local public school districts and operated as public schools, with religious instruction offered outside regular school hours. Although in Poughkeepsie, for example, the arrangement survived for a quarter of a century, it was eventually abandoned, because of the legal and constitutional objections of non-Catholics, and theological and philosophical ones by Catholics. So the idea of a Catholic program fully integrated into public education today is still no more than an idea, and is likely to remain so in the foreseeable future. We shall, however, return to the proposal later in this discussion.

But whatever arrangements might be worked out in the future for integrating Catholic schools into the American school system, Catholic schools will remain necessary—necessary to both society and to the Church. Let us now see why this is so.

Catholic Schools and Society

Many facts, figures and theoretical arguments have been advanced in favor of the service rendered by Catholic schools to society. That they do render a service, in that they now enroll five million American children and young people annually, is beyond dispute. In recent years the dispute has been, rather, about the quality and the effects of the education offered. Rhetoric on the subject has flowed freely; conclusive facts have been much harder to come by. As Michael O'Neill has shown in a recent survey (*How Good Are Catholic Schools?*, Dayton, 1968), the studies made thus far are generally deficient in one or more respects, and their findings have been mutually contradictory. Thus, in some studies Catholic school students appear somewhat superior academically to public school students; in others, they appear somewhat inferior. One frequent accusation against Catholic schools—that they contribute to social divisiveness—has, however, been laid to rest rather conclusively by Greeley and Rossi. According to their findings, those who have attended Catholic schools as a rule are better able to accept people of different backgrounds and to fit into society as a whole than Catholics who attend public schools. They are, for example, as likely as public-school Catholics to be involved in community affairs and to have non-Catholic friends, visitors, neighbors and co-workers; and they were found to be somewhat more open-minded in their attitudes concerning civil liberties. There was also at least some evidence that the younger and better educated Catholic school Catholics were more tolerant and socially conscious than were Catholics of the same age and educational level who had not attended Catholic schools. None of the differences were as significant as the Catholic school supporter might like, but they were nonetheless measurable and real.

In short—to state the case with a minimum of rhetoric—it seems safe to say that Catholic schools do at least a satisfactory job of producing competent, well-motivated and productive citizens. It seems, too, that Catholic schools do not contribute to "divisiveness" in society but may in fact help counteract tendencies in this direction.

Catholic schools also make a direct economic contribution to American society, quite apart from the economic contribution their graduates can be expected to make. Although the complexities of the situation make precise figures impossible, this contribution is evidently very substantial. Put simply, it would amount to whatever it would cost the government to educate the approximately five million students enrolled annually in Catholic schools (less the assistance they now receive or expect to receive from public funds). This figure at present would probably amount to $3 or $4 billion a year in operating costs alone, quite apart from the capital expenditures that would also be required to accommodate those students in public schools.

Many Americans do not seem to have grasped the fiscal

implications of closing down Catholic and other private schools. For example, early in 1969 former Governor George Romney, in a message to the people of Michigan before going to Washington to become Secretary of Housing and Urban Development, suggested that religious groups "leave secular education to the state" and concentrate exclusively on "religious and moral instruction." At the time, the issue of expanded public assistance to nonpublic education was being debated throughout the state. Romney argued that state aid to nonpublic schools would be expensive, and "I don't believe taxpayers will support such a costly system." But as was immediately pointed out, it would have been even more expensive to the taxpayers of Michigan to absorb the state's 330,000 nonpublic school students into public schools. One estimate was $200 million annually in operating funds, along with $1 billion for facilities.

The picture is similar in other states and localities with large concentrations of nonpublic school children. In a detailed study, prepared in 1969 for the Massachusetts Advisory Council on Education, André L. Danière of Boston College and George F. Madaus of the New England Catholic Education Center computed the cost to the state and local communities of a gradual phasing-out of Catholic schools in Massachusetts, and of transferring their students to public schools. According to Danière and Madaus, over the ten-year period from 1969–70 to 1978–79, the consequent addition to public expenditures in the state would amount to $1.789 billion, or an average annual expenditure of $179 million. Similarly, in June 1969 the Committee on Education of the New York archdiocese, noting that Catholic school enrollment in the archdiocese was 216,000, estimated that operating expenses for New York City would be increased by some $200 million a year if there were no Catholic schools (assuming a cost per pupil of about $1,000 in city public schools), and that the expenses of other municipalities in the archdiocese would be increased by another $100 million (assuming a cost per pupil of about $850). In 1958, as we have seen, Roger Freeman estimated that the added cost to public schools of enrolling all the nonpublic school children of the nation would amount to nearly $4 billion by 1970. (In a statement made in 1965 before a Senate education subcommittee, Freeman estimated that nonpublic schools were then saving taxpayers $3.5 billion a year in operating costs alone, apart from capital expenditures.)

Even supposing that Catholic schools were totally subsidized out of public funds for all "secular" aspects of their program, the cost to taxpayers would apparently still be less than it would be to educate all Catholic-school students in public schools. The reason, as noted in our chapter on finances, is that costs per pupil in Catholic schools are substantially lower than in public schools (chiefly because of the presence in Catholic schools of religious teachers and the absence of a large centralized administrative staff).

Thus, Catholic schools make a contribution to American society through educating a substantial number of citizens and through savings to taxpayers. These contributions are important, and deserve wider recognition than they have up to now received. But the schools render, in addition, a far more important service to society—that of guarding, both in principle and in practice, diversity and freedom of choice in education.

In the first place, Catholic schools represent competition for public schools—not the cutthroat competition of two institutions each trying to outgrab the other in getting money and students, but the fruitful competition of self-improvement. As long as Catholic and other private schools go on trying to increase the excellence of their programs, they provide an added and possibly necessary incentive for public schools to do the same (just as, of course, the betterment of public schools calls for a parallel effort by nonpublic schools). Competition of this sort is valuable for all concerned and is also in accord with American tradition.

Beyond this, Catholic schools also represent an opportunity—though one that admittedly is underexploited—for experiment in educational methods. Vested interests certainly exist in Catholic education, and there are sensitivities—apparently on the increase—in the Catholic community; and the Catholic school is and should be answerable to the community it serves. For these reasons it would be reckless to suggest that the Catholic school is totally autonomous, and thus free (quite apart from limitations of vision and of resources) to experiment and innovate at will. But at least, as compared with American public schools, Catholic schools are relatively unhampered by bureaucratic red tape and relatively less inhibited by political pressures and by the idiosyncrasies of fringe elements. This situation gives a rather wide latitude for experiment with new methods and structures. Catholic schools quite properly have been criticized for their failure to make more imaginative use of this opportunity (although in fairness the practical problem of survival in the face of shortages in funds and personnel must be acknowledged). But they remain potentially a laboratory for imaginative thinking and practice, and in this respect too the nation would be poorer without them.

More fundamentally, however, Catholic schools are important because they ensure that there will not be an educational monopoly in America. A single public system of schools would mean a departure from the American tradition of educational pluralism—a departure that could have disturbing consequences. People should have the right to choose—among products and also among ideas. There are laws to prevent business monopolies and restraint of trade, as well as to guarantee freedom of speech—a freedom important both to the one who expresses his ideas and to the public that hears and judges them. Monopoly is at variance with the American way of doing things. Not only is there the prospect that the monopolist will abuse his advantage; the very existence of a monopoly tends to reduce the options available and thereby to diminish the practical exercise of freedom. This holds true no matter how scrupulous and even high-minded the monopolist may be.

The idea of monopoly in education is peculiarly abhorrent. Here the values at stake are of an entirely different and higher order than whether an automobile buyer shall have the option of choosing among the products of one or several automobile manufacturers. They belong to the moral and intellectual order, and in these areas of life the exercise of free choice is pre-eminently important. It is essential that this possibility not be merely negative (that is, the absence of coercion) or theoretical; there must, rather, be the possibility of genuine, practical free choice. So far as education is concerned, this means that Americans should have both the right and the opportunity to choose from among diverse schools and school systems—and that non-public schools must make up more than a "token" system, but must be numerous enough to accommodate parents and students who choose this kind of school. The Catholic school is an institutional embodiment of this right and opportunity. In the field of education it helps to flesh out the principle of freedom of choice. In the past century millions of Catholic Americans have demonstrated their urgent desire for precisely this institutional embodiment of freedom of choice in education; millions more are doing so today. Their instinct is sound, based as it is not only on religious conviction or denominational loyalty but also on the American commitment to allowing the broadest possible latitude to freedom of choice consistent with the well being of society.

Thomas F. Green of the Educational Policy Research Center at Syracuse University has recently suggested four broad categories into which schools may be divided according to the predominant values they tend to foster: managerial (with the usefulness of the "product" to society, especially its economic and military aspects, the chief criterion of value); traditional (designed to "preserve a collective memory," and a continuity between past, present and future); humanistic (with the aim of promoting the maximum development of each individual); and religious (whose task is to "nurture a form of consciousness in which the individual sees his relation to others as mediated by The Holy"). Although schools in this country generally profess humanistic objectives, Green suggests that the predominant model, especially in American public education, is in fact managerial. He sees, furthermore, little likelihood of a change in the foreseeable future. It is not our intention to argue here that the managerial form of education is necessarily bad—or to suggest that nonpublic schools, including Catholic ones, have not themselves in many ways adopted it as a model. However, the schools whose aim is traditional, humanistic or religious do embody important values; and if Green is right in supposing that public schools will of necessity remain committed to managerial education, it would seem to be the special task of the nonpublic schools to embody and promote these alternative educational values in American society. Indeed, it would seem that a far stronger conscious effort should be made in this direction than has been made to date.

At the same time, it should also be said that a greater degree of integration of the Catholic school into the total American educational effort would also appear desirable, provided it can be accomplished without sacrificing the special functions and purposes of Catholic education. One can only speak in general and speculative terms here, but it would be a happy thing if the "Catholic" school, while retaining its full and distinct identity as Catholic, could also be regarded as—and become—a component of the "public" educational system.

The idea is not so far-fetched as it may sound. There is, after all, a real sense in which the "Catholic" school is already a "public" school. But acknowledgment of this is slow in coming. A major part of the difficulty lies in the ready assumption that the public school in its present form is the only possible expression of the American genius in education. But it would be more accurate to say that the special American contribution to education has been, not *public* education precisely, but rather *universal* education—the commitment to educating all citizens, in every stratum of society. This being so, the "Catholic" school is as fully "American" in its inspiration and commitment as any other.

One may hope, then, for a day when Catholic and public educators will seek a genuine *rapprochement;* when the concept of "public" education will be broadened to embrace a genuine pluralism, and schools operating under a wide variety of auspices, denominational and otherwise, and embodying a wide variety of educational values and methods, can be welcomed as equal partners into the "public" system of education, meanwhile remaining free to pursue their own special purposes; and when conceptual agreement will be embodied practically in the sharing of ideas, skills, personnel, funds and facilities. Legal and constitutional difficulties stand in the way of such developments at the present time; even more important, perhaps, are ingrained patterns of thought and behavior that make such concerted activity difficult, if not impossible. Stranger things have come to pass, however, and apparently insuperable obstacles have been known to diminish under the impact of good sense and good will. One can hope, if not expect, that sooner or later this is what will happen to education in America.

Catholic Schools and the People of God

It is possible only in the abstract to make a neat and simple distinction between the services rendered by the Catholic school to the civic and the Christian communities. The Catholic school's mission of service, after all, embodied not so much in ideas or even in institutions as in persons, and to sift out all the motivations of Catholic educators would be at best a somewhat futile enterprise. The Catholic school is in much the same position as other church-related institutions and programs—hospitals and social welfare agencies, for example—which witness to the desire of the Church and its members to contribute to human betterment. The categories of "secular" and "religious" education, under which Catholic schools and their purposes are frequently discussed, tend to falsify, through abstraction, the often complex motivation of those involved.

Bearing in mind at once the essential witness of the Catholic school and the complexity of its operation, it nevertheless is still possible to point to ways in which it serves the special purposes of the Church, the People of God. Perhaps the most important of these is the reinforcement of specifically Christian and Catholic values. The operative word here is "reinforcement." A school, it seems, does not ordinarily originate the values its students hold; it can, however, be quite effective in developing, through ordered experience and intellectual exploration, the values implanted and fostered by the parents at home.

Supporters of Catholic schools have in the past frequently cast their defense in the form of an attack on the motives or ideology of public school educators. This is as unfair as it is impolitic. Public schools have made and continue to make an enormous contribution to American society. The dedication and competence of public school educators are realities for which all Americans, Catholics included, can be grateful. It is a mistake, too, to speak of the public school system, as some Catholics have done, as a monolithic enterprise. There is substantial decentralization in public education and diversity in public school programs from one community and one region of the country to another. The values of particular regional and ethnic groups are represented *de facto* in the public schools—appropriately so. And where they are not (as black Americans in many places are now complaining), community pressures generally succeed sooner or later in bringing about changes in the schools to incorporate the values desired by the community.

It is also a fact that public schools teach important and highly desirable values. Concepts like brotherhood, citizenship, honesty and fair play have a part in the public school program, and it is evident that the schools have real success in inculcating these values in their students. To speak of the public schools as if they were insensitive to ethical values or ineffective in fostering them does not square with the facts.

Despite all this, however, it remains true that public schools are, by judicial fiat if not community consensus, monolithically alike in their exclusion from the school program of specifically religious values and the religious dimension of human experience. Value-free education does not exist, since values of one kind or another are inevitably conveyed by the very process of education. Thus, it can be argued, by omitting certain areas of human experience from their program, the public schools "teach," implicitly at least, that these are matters of no great importance and can reasonably and safely be passed over by the student. Unlike other groups in society, furthermore, religious groups have no possibility of obtaining redress for this situation, since a firmly held legal and judicial tradition bars the introduction of specifically religious values, concepts and attitudes into the public school.

A closer look makes clear the radical deficiency (from the point of view of the religious believer) of public education in its present form. Not only are public schools positively forbidden to teach specifically religious values, but they must of necessity offer—at least by implication—a false and objectionable rationale for the values they *do* teach. Thus, for the religious believer, the problem with the public schools is not simply the absence of something desirable (religious values) but, as is more to the point, the presence of something undesirable (a false rationale for values).

Public schools are, for example, generally committed to teaching "brotherhood." All well and good; it is commendable that the public schools should encourage their students to believe in and practice so excellent a concept. From a Christian point of view, however, it is clear that the ultimate explanation of why brotherhood is important—why, in fact, it is a value at all—is rooted in the universal Fatherhood of God; that is to say, all men are created by the same God, and thus stand in essentially the same relation to Him and to one another. But what explanation is the public school permitted to give for brotherhood? Presumably it can say nothing about the Fatherhood of God (if it does so, it is violating the command of the highest court in the country). It must then teach, by silence if in no other way, that brotherhood is either a self-evident value requiring no explanation above and beyond itself (which simply is not true) or that brotherhood is important because it helps to cement society together and make it possible for the members of society to get along with each other (which is true, but only part of the truth, and thus from a religious point of view quite inadequate).

The same holds true of other values taught and encouraged in the public school. The public school is obliged to offer either no rationale for these values or an explanation that from the Christian point of view is at best partially true, and therefore inadequate. In their handling of values, public schools must therefore be judged deficient by the religious believer.

There are, in short, two aspects of the problem: the public school is obliged, first, to omit from its program the whole religious dimension of human experience, and second, to suggest an inadequate and—from the Christian point of view—false rationale for the values it does teach, however commendable these values may be in themselves. Thus, in its approach to the entire religious, ethical and spiritual dimension of life, the public school can never do more than a partial job of education; and, to the extent that its program implies a secular-humanist system of values inimical to supernatural religion, it may do actual harm.

The reader may ask why so much stress has been laid here on the rationale for values. A common-sense view of the matter would suggest that if the public schools do in fact encourage their students to believe in and practice something as important as brotherhood, it is hair-splitting to ask whether the schools have also given them an adequate basis for accepting this value. Surely, according to this view, it is more important that young people (or those of any age) accept a value like brotherhood than that they have a philosophically and theologically adequate reason for doing so. And if parents or the churches feel that the public schools are not providing students with such reasons, do they not remain perfectly free to supplement the public school program as they see fit?

To take the second point first, the question would seem to be one not of supplementing what is taught about values in the public school but of counteracting it. If this analysis is correct, public schools are in fact teaching a rationale for values, and the rationale is not acceptable to religious believers. Making up for a deficiency in the public school program would be hard enough, but to correct what one is obliged to regard as false teaching in that program is even harder, and is not an undertaking that any parent or educator can look forward to with enthusiasm.

As for the argument that it is much more important that a person believe in and practice a value like brotherhood (or honesty or good citizenship) than that he have a totally adequate reason for doing so, this is undeniably true but it misses the long-range implications of the matter. Values without a rationale—or with a weak or false rationale—are imperiled. They may be held to for a generation or perhaps several generations, but over a period of time their defective intellectual foundation must be seen for what it is. When this happens, it becomes necessary that a new and adequate rationale be developed, or there will be a collapse of the value system. The current confusion and conflict over values in American society suggests that both may now be happening at once, and at this stage it would be foolhardy to predict whether the eventual outcome of the process will be such a collapse or the achievement of a new consensus.

Admittedly (and regrettably) the foregoing analysis is stated in the negative terms of a critique of public education —though not of the motives of public school educators. This is unfortunately necessary, since there is no way of making the point we wish to make without citing the radical deficiency of public education in regard to the teaching of values. The matter can, however, also be stated positively: if public schools teach an inadequate or false rationale for values, Catholic schools can teach (at least in the Catholic view of things) an adequate and correct rationale for values. This is not to say that Catholic school educators are any more high-minded, any more dedicated, any more ethically sensitive than public school educators. But in doing what the public school, because of legal and judicial doctrine, is forbidden to do, the Catholic school finds its distinctive reason for existence.

The Catholic school does not of course find its reason for existence simply in providing students with a cut-and-dried "rationale" for values. What the Catholic school does, ideally, is to offer the opportunity for a searching exploration of religious values and beliefs; ideally, too, it does so in a structured setting—a school community—where these values are lived out as well.

It cannot be said that every Catholic school lives up to this description. Obviously, what is being described is an ideal for Catholic education. In practice, Catholic schools often fall short of the ideal—sometimes tragically so—as, for instance, in those high schools that have expelled girls who get pregnant, lest they "scandalize" other students, and in schools that blandly perpetuate *de facto* segregation while paying lip service to racial justice. Yet many also succeed. It is worth noting that many of the severest critics of Catholic schools, who complain of an inadequate commitment to social values, are themselves products of such schools, and are as likely as not to have acquired their own sense of commitment there. Only in the Catholic school is it even possible to strive for full realization of the ideal of Catholic education. Catholic schools provide a situation within which the effort can be made, and this in itself is a reason for their existence.

The school, of course—Catholic, public or whatever—is by no means the only medium by which values are transmitted to the young. Other agencies, primarily the family, are also of vital importance. Children acquire their first and probably their most lasting indoctrination in a value system from their parents, and not so much from what their parents tell them as from the way in which the parents live out, or fail to live out, the values they profess. Nevertheless, it would be false to conclude from this that the school occupies a peripheral or easily dispensable role in the process of value formation. On the contrary, one is obliged to agree with Kenneth Boulding that formal education plays at least as important a role in socialization as do the family and the peer group. The same conclusion emerges from the research of Greeley and Rossi, who found that the *combination* of Catholic school with practicing Catholic parents made a significant difference in the religious values and practice of the products of Catholic education. In discussing the function of the school in socialization, Boulding goes so far as to say that the public school has become a kind of "church" for the modern state, serving as an instrument for transmitting desirable social and civic values to the young. If this is so, it would seem at least equally necessary that religious groups have available to them schools that can transmit their own particular value system to their young people.

Seen in this way, the Catholic school is an indispensable extension and reinforcement of the Catholic family. Something like this is suggested by those Catholic parents who offer "discipline" as a reason for sending their children to Catholic schools. "Discipline" is admittedly a vague word, and for some people it may in fact mean no more than regimentation or the old-fashioned dictum of "spare the rod and spoil the child." It seems likely, however, that Catholic parents who speak of valuing the "discipline" of Catholic schools in fact refer to a whole constellation of attitudes and behavior, centered about a coherent system of values—one that continues in a broader setting, what they as parents are trying to accomplish within the circle of the family. It is by no means unrealistic or unworthy for parents to expect this of the school. On the contrary, their expectation represents a valid insight into the role of the school in the process of socialization.

Inevitably, of course, there remains the question whether

the Catholic school alone can satisfy the expectations of parents who are concerned with the reinforcement of Catholic values. One must note, specifically, the tremendous financial and human burden placed on the Catholic community that must support these schools; the availability of out-of-school religious education programs, and the possibility of improving them significantly if some of the resources now devoted to Catholic schools were to be invested in them; the growing importance, in the view of Catholic educators, of adult religious education; and the disappearance from the public schools of anti-Catholic proselytizing. In view of all these things, the argument goes, it would make more sense at the present time to give up the effort to continue Catholic schools and concentrate instead on other means of religious instruction and formation.

Each of these considerations deserves a serious answer. We have already concluded that the public schools are not wholly satisfactory, and may indeed be quite unsatisfactory, in their handling of values. Granted that the public schools are no longer "Protestant"; but neither are they "Christian" nor even "religious," and moreover they cannot be, in the view of the courts. Nor can the public schools be described as religiously "neutral," since, as we have seen, they inevitably teach, by implication at least, a rationale for the values that is not acceptable from a religious point of view.

Concerning adult religious education, one can agree that this field has been neglected and is urgently in need of attention, without concluding that the religious education of children is therefore of less importance. Research on education, notably in the Coleman Report, the government's massive study of the disadvantaged, emphasizes that the earliest years are crucial for the development of attitudes and skills. New approaches to the religious education of children certainly need to be explored—approaches that put less emphasis on rote formulas, and more on deepened insight and experience. This, however, is a very different thing from emphasizing the education of adults at the expense of children. Christianity, we are told, is a "religion for adults." Obviously, that is true. But religious educators who use this slogan as an argument for de-emphasizing Catholic schools seem not to have thought through the implications of their own rhetoric. How, after all, do adults acquire their religious attitudes and beliefs except by a long formational process beginning in the earliest childhood years? How can adult religious education be really effective unless it builds on an already established foundation of knowledge and attitudes? The argument for adult religious education is in fact also an argument for Catholic schools.

But cannot the religious education of children and young people be safely entrusted to other agencies—the home, the parish (especially the parish liturgy), and religious instruction outside of school? In reply, one can only cite again the crucial role of the school in socialization and in the transmission of values. Parents should certainly take a more active role in the religious education of their children; the liturgy should be examined and revised with the aim of making it a more effective instrument of education and formation; and non-school programs of religious education deserve all possible support. As we have suggested earlier, a way of upgrading them would be to integrate them into the overall Catholic educational program rather than treat them as poor relations, as is so often done at present. But none of these is or can be a substitute for the schools, because none of them can possibly provide the total environment of a school.

There is a special difficulty—the reader may already have sensed it—in trying to speak in this context of out-of-school religious education. It should be obvious by now that we do not regard such programs as adequate substitutes for Catholic schools. The practical difficulties alone are all but insurmountable—fatigued and bored children, harassed parents and/or instructors—and perhaps even more serious are the psychological problems, especially the possibility that religious education in these circumstances may come to be identified in the student's mind with piano lessons, ice-skating classes and other fringe educational experiences. But we are nevertheless convinced, as we have said frequently, that out-of-school religious education programs deserve much more attention and interest and a far larger share of the available resources of money and manpower than they have received up to now—if for no other reason than that the number of Catholic children who are clients of these programs is increasing year by year and these children deserve as good a religious education as is possible in the circumstances.

We believe that the best hope for the improvement of out-of-school programs lies in tying them more closely to the schools, through developing the sort of unified education program described earlier. To an increasing extent Catholic schools must become active centers of Christian education for the entire community. While offering full school programs for as many children and young people as they can accommodate and still maintain a high level of academic quality, they must also broaden their scope to provide more and better programs for children and adults who do not attend Catholic schools. Working out the details will not be an easy task, but will require intelligent planning; in particular situations, Catholic "schools" may have to be converted into Catholic "education centers." The details of such plans must take local situations into account, and cannot be made into a blueprint beforehand. It can be said with assurance, however, that a mass closing of Catholic schools would be no solution to the problem of providing religious education for the total Catholic community. The predictable result would be confusion, chaos, and ultimate disaster for religious education, whether in or outside of school.

Some Catholic critics appear to assume that religious practice is the only significant outcome of religious education. If this were true, the Catholic school would probably not be essential. Most members of the Church could probably acquire the habit of attending Mass and receiving the sacraments through other means. But only the most rigid anti-intellectualism can now be satisfied with a "religion" that stops there. There is an intellectual content to "religion" which can and should be taught. Not to teach it would be to contribute to the religious illiteracy of Catholics so often decried in the past, and would be intolerable in the present time of change and confusion in the Church.

Current efforts to expand and strengthen counseling programs on both the elementary and secondary levels cannot be considered a substitute for religious education. Counseling is one aspect of the educational program, but only one. A good counselor, available at the right time, can correct mistaken attitudes and concepts, help review what a student already knows, and even have a decisive influence on the student's course of action. He cannot expect, however, to give an entire course in Catholic doctrine, and no one can suppose he should. The proposal to make priests and religious available as counselors to Catholic students attending public schools would offer many advantages, and this should be done wherever possible. But given the inherent limitations of counseling, it can hardly be a substitute for the religious education program of the Catholic school, as the well-trained counselor would be the first to admit.

Many current writers on religious education have called for an emphasis on religious experience and commitment as a desirable part of a total religious education program. But religious understanding—the intellectual component—should likewise not be neglected. This is not to say that the special task of the Catholic school is to teach "about" religion, but rather that it can provide a rounded program of religious education, encompassing religious understanding, religious experience and religious commitment. The focal person in this enterprise is the teacher, who can demonstrate by precept and example what it means to hold a coherent set of values and beliefs, and at the same time offer a rationale for these that can withstand rigorous intellectual examination. The student requires a forum and a community in which his own emerging convictions, doubts and speculations can be tested, and this is what the Catholic school provides. Even if Catholic parents had the time and the skill to do the same (and generally they do not), their effort could not be totally integrated into the child's school life in a manner that would continue and perfect what they are trying to accomplish.

This, it should be noted, is not precisely the same thing as "permeation"—the idea that a religious atmosphere or influence somehow pervades all aspects of the Catholic school program. The word we prefer to use is, rather, "integration"—a rounded program to encompass religious understanding, experience and commitment. Only in the Catholic school is this possible.

A final objection to the Catholic school deserves to be noted here, not because it is valid but because it is heard increasingly among Catholics. This is the argument that maintaining the schools has led to a serious imbalance in the allocation of Church resources for education. In the words of one recent critic, distributive justice calls for "the abandonment of [the Church's] present school system (which serves only a small percentage of Catholics and indeed only a part of those of school age) in favor of a new educational structure which serves *all* Catholics of every age and station."

Certainly no one would disagree with the proposition that the Church should adopt the educational structure than comes nearest to serving "all Catholics of every age and station." (And why "Catholics" only? Why not all men?) But in our estimation, it is precisely the Catholic school that can best do this. To be sure, Catholic schools enroll only a part of the Catholic school-age population; still, it implies a very limited vision of schooling to suppose that a school serves only those who happen to be enrolled in it. Do public schools "serve" only the children whom they enroll? If so, a very persuasive argument could be made that only the parents of those children should pay to support the schools. But the argument is based on an obvious fallacy. The public schools serve not only the children they enroll, but the total community *through* the students who are educated.

The same is true of Catholic schools. They serve the total community through the students who are educated, and they also serve the total Catholic community by developing in their students understanding of and commitment to a Christian system of values. Admittedly, Catholic schools still need to find ways of increasing this service. How they can do so is to a great extent the subject of this book. But it should be reiterated that Catholic schools do far more than serve only the students they enroll. Catholic schools do indeed serve their students directly; but through their students they go on to serve the Catholic community and the total community. This is the way in which any school—public, private or church-related—carries out its role of service, and it seems oddly short-sighted to ignore that fact in the sole case of Catholic schools. To date, the Catholic school has been a highly effective medium through which the Church has exercised its educational mission. With imagination and courage, the Catholic school can become more effective than it has ever been before, expanding its direct service to encompass, for example, Catholic adults and Catholic children enrolled in public schools. Thus it would be a tragedy if a curious blindness—a "numbers" mentality equating enrollment with service—were now to be used as a rationale for withdrawing resources from Catholic schools at a time when the Catholic community and the civic community both stand in urgent need of them.

We have here been setting out a high and difficult goal

for the Catholic school. But Catholic schools have achieved it in the past and are achieving it today—all too imperfectly in many cases but with surprising success in others. Catholic schools are a tremendous burden for the Catholic community, but they are also a tremendous opportunity and an indispensable instrument for Christian education. Given these facts, the only conclusion possible is that the burden must continue to be borne—and, we might add, borne gratefully.

7 Schools for the Future

NOT many years ago, the question that is now being asked—whether Catholic schools have a future—would have been unthinkable. Catholic schools occupied the same impregnable position as fish on Friday and the Latin Mass. But both of these are now things of the past. Changes in the Church that no one would have considered possible only a decade ago are accomplished facts today. Likewise, the disappearance of Catholic schools can no longer be dismissed as unthinkable. That they exist now is no guarantee that they will continue to do so.

Catholic schools will in fact probably *not* continue to exist (or not in anything like their present numbers) unless they undergo the changes necessary to ensure and to justify their existence. In previous chapters we have suggested some areas in which these changes must occur: organization and policy-making, fund-raising and budgeting, the recruitment and status of teachers. None of these changes will be easy; some may entail personal anguish and institutional dislocation. But unless they are forthcoming, and soon—that is, within the next five years—there is real danger that the Catholic school system in the United States will find itself trapped in an all but irreversible process of decline. The future of Catholic schools is certain to be very different from their past, since to maintain the status quo is today not only undesirable but impossible. Change is the order of the day in American society, and Catholic education will inevitably be part of this process. The only real question is whether the change in Catholic schools will be chaotic and unplanned, or whether it will be carried out in a rational manner to serve the best interests of the Church and American society.

One of the worst kept secrets in Catholic education at present is that the educators are running scared. Lack of planning for change is mainly responsible for the atmosphere of uncertainty that prevails in Catholic educational circles. Changes are needed—everyone recognizes that; but because not enough serious thought has been given to the form these changes are to take, many of those on the firing line in classrooms and administrators' offices have reached a state approaching panic, or even despair.

Two things are necessary in planning for the Catholic schools of the future: first, an adequate restatement of goals, and second, structures for achieving them.

Goals for the Future

The restatement of goals is crucial. Catholic schools in the past were judged a success, despite their manifest problems and weaknesses, largely because there was a true consensus in the Catholic community as to what they should be doing, and that was what the schools proceeded to do. This consensus remained largely unformulated, but it was real, and thus it was the heart and soul of the Catholic school system. The purpose of the schools, it was generally agreed, was to form their students into good Catholics and good citizens, as both were understood by the Catholic community. A "good Catholic" was one who kept the Commandments, who regularly took part in the sacramental life of the Church and attended Mass on Sunday, who contributed to the support of the Church and was docile toward authority. The standard, in short, was one of rather minimal observance, and if the possibility of a higher ideal was acknowledged, it was generally regarded as the concern of the priests and sisters; the ordinary layman (that is, the ordinary product of the Catholic schools) need not trouble himself with *that*. In saying this we do not mean to be either patronizing or presumptuous, as if it were somehow possible to measure the spiritual accomplishments of prior generations of American Catholics. We are speaking rather of the outward manifestations of spirituality; and in these matters we believe it fair to say that the standard set by American Catholicism in the past was one of "minimal observance."

The notion of the good citizen was similarly limited: He paid his taxes, he obeyed the law, he fought his country's wars and, in peacetime, made his modest contribution by performing, dependably and unspectacularly, the tasks allotted to him by his particular job and state in life. He took society pretty much as he found it, living within the framework of its values and offering only marginal criticism or pressure for change and improvement. The Catholic response to the race question is typical of this uncritical and passive attitude. In retrospect it becomes shocking that generations of American Catholics, many of them graduates of Catholic schools, could have tolerated (and often, indeed, supported) both attitudes and structures that condemned an entire group of their fellow citizens to permanent second-class status. Yet this is what happened, and it stands as an indictment of the goals proposed and sought by Catholic schools, along with other institutions of the Church and of society.

Nevertheless, it remains a fact that what the schools were expected to do, they did well. Catholic schools did produce "good Catholics" and "good citizens" according to the approved model. If the model now appears deficient, the fault was not entirely with the schools.

Today it is still possible to sum up the goal of the Catholic school as the formation of good Catholics and good citizens. But the concepts themselves have altered so radically that it is necessary for the schools to make a corresponding adjustment. This, however, is a very different thing from abandoning the schools entirely. The American Catholic school system represents an enormous resource for achieving the new goals of the contemporary Catholic community. The present challenge is twofold: to clarify these goals, and to make the adaptations in the schools that will achieve them most effectively. Admittedly this is no small order; but those who argue for the abandonment of Catholic schools are in reality asking the Church to handicap itself by giving up an effective instrument for creating the new model Christian that the times demand. If the schools should disappear, there is nothing even remotely visible on the horizon that could take their place. The proposal that the schools be phased out seems more often to arise from self-hatred—or repudiation of one's past, which amounts to the same thing—than from reasoned analysis. American Catholics find it difficult to come to terms with their past; seeking to shed their origins, they tend also to reject the institutions, notably the schools, that they identify with those origins. But this is a dangerous thing to do. Institutions—all romanticizing aside—are essential to any society, and American Catholics would be far wiser to spend their energies in redirecting the goals of existing institutions than in destroying what could only with difficulty, if at all, be replaced.

Certainly this is pre-eminently true of the schools. If their goals are to be redirected, the process will almost certainly begin with a recognition that the Catholic school exists to teach a "this-worldly other-worldliness," in keeping with Vatican II's Constitution on the Church in the Modern World. The Church, in the words of that document (§ 40), "serves as a leaven and as a kind of soul for human society."

The Church "not only communicates divine life to man, but in some way casts reflected light of that life over the entire earth." Thus, "through her individual members and her whole community, the Church believes she can contribute greatly toward making the family of man and its history more human." The pre-eminent role of the Catholic school is to further this vision of a Church immersed in human affairs but bringing to them at the same time a spiritual dimension and an orientation toward the heavenly city.

This will mean that the Catholic school must develop in its students a commitment to the welfare, both material and spiritual, of other human beings. The Catholic school can no longer settle for the "good Catholic" and his minimal observance, or the "good citizen" whose social vision is bounded by the status quo. The graduates of the Catholic schools of the future must be infused with a permanent sense of apostolic commitment. "Revolution" is for some a daring word, but there is a legitimate sense in which Catholic schools must seek to form revolutionaries. The message of Christianity is itself radical and even revolutionary, and the mature Christian is a man in a state of permanent revolution—a revolution that begins within himself but extends to the society in which he lives. In this sense Catholic education should be dedicated to the training of revolutionaries, men who are remade in and by Christ, and who then go on, through peaceful means, to remake society.

The goals of the Catholic school must encompass the eradication of racism and poverty in this country. They must go beyond national boundaries to include a commitment to international justice and peace. Catholic schools should consciously seek to form Christians who will be notable for their work in the Peace Corps, in VISTA and in the other service-oriented professions and groups, public and private, that have appeared in recent years. Catholic schools should also seek to instill in their students a commitment to such church-related apostolic groups as the Extension Volunteers and the Papal Volunteers for Latin America. And of course the schools ought, as in the past, to foster vocations to permanent apostolic service in the priesthood and religious life.

The revolution in catechetical materials that is now in progress reflects this new thrust in Catholic education. Inevitably, mistakes have been made, but the new materials are a welcome sign of a new and healthy emphasis on the Christian's role in society. In the words of one catechetical writer, "The authors are attempting positively to communicate to students that they are primarily members of the human family and responsible for one another." And another writer, reviewing some of the dominant themes in the new materials, has asked:

> Is it too much to expect, then, that the new society of believers will be hallmarked by a genuine love for the brethren of different origins, colors, cultures, and creeds? That future Christians will be truly Catholic, meaning universal, occupied more with setting up self-help projects in the barrios of South America than with raising funds for an air-conditioned neighborhood gym? .... That they might be willing to die for citizens instead of state, or live for Christians more than for an institution?

By consciously setting for itself such goals as these, the Catholic school of the future will transcend the charge—heard these days with some frequency—that it represents an "elitist" approach to education. The Catholic school *must* in fact be an elite school, but the word requires careful definition. Catholic education should foster an elite based on apostolic commitment, a corps of wholehearted Christians; and this must be its chief goal, not its marginal, diffidently hoped-for by-product.

In order to realize this objective, the Catholic school of

the future may need to devote less time to formal religion "classes" and more to other religious programs that give an opportunity to live out the meaning of Christian life. The liturgy in the school must be revitalized—not by having more compulsory exercises but rather through intelligent experiment. (And this, it might be added, should go a good deal further than guitars at Mass.) In the same vein, the school should help its students to live their religion through carefully planned and supervised social action projects—inner-city tutoring, work with the retarded and handicapped, all sorts of summer projects. Some of this is already being done in Catholic schools, but it needs to be expanded and made an integral part of the educational program.

The Catholic school of the future probably ought to be less child-centered than it has been up to now. Not that Catholic schools can or should de-emphasize the training of young children; recent research on the process of learning merely confirms that education in the earliest years has the greatest impact, not merely on intellectual development but on value formation as well. Granting this, Catholic schools should nevertheless be extended to serve other segments of the Christian community. Catholic schools must become vigorous centers for adult education, directed both to lay Catholics and to priests and religious. (In-service training programs for priests, brothers and sisters, it might be remarked, are urgently needed at the present time.)

Catholic schools should also extend themselves to serve the poor and underprivileged of American society. A cutback of the Catholic school commitment to the innercity would be a tragedy for scores of American communities, placing an additional burden on the already hard-pressed public school system. It would also mean defaulting by the Church on a long-term commitment to parents and students. It would eliminate an important resource for experiment and innovation in educating the disadvantaged. And, per-

haps most important of all, it would deprive the inner city
of an ideological and spiritual commitment which that sector of American society sorely needs. In the inner cities, as
everywhere else, the Catholic school should consciously
work toward the goal of forming apostolic Christian leaders.

Just how large a contribution Catholic education can
make *directly* toward solving inner-city problems is, however, still far from clear. In 1968, Monsignor James C. Donohue, director of the Division of Elementary and Secondary Education, U. S. Catholic Conference, proposed a new
set of priorities for Catholic education, in an article that has
been widely discussed. The first priority, he said, should be
the operation of excellent Catholic schools for the poor and
disadvantaged of the inner city; the second, expanded and
improved religious education for Catholics; and the third,
to whatever extent the remaining resources would permit,
the operation of Catholic schools for middle-class Catholic
children. At the convention of the National Catholic Educational Association in April 1968 at San Francisco, Harold
Howe II, who was then U. S. Commissioner of Education,
also argued that the first priority of Catholic schools should
be the inner city. He listed three characteristics of the Catholic school system that equipped it for the task: first, that it
is "mainly metropolitan in nature . . . concentrated in the
major cities and their suburbs;" second, that it "operates
outside the political system that sometimes prevents public
school superintendents from doing what they know to be
the wisest thing for education;" and third, that Catholic
dioceses (and thus Catholic school systems) "comprise both
cities and suburbs, thus permitting a metropolitan approach
to educational problems."

The arguments and proposals advanced by Monsignor
Donohue and by Commissioner Howe deserve not only to be
seriously considered, but to be acted upon. Whether or not

the inner city can be the first area of emphasis remains an open question, however.

Basically the issue is whether the limited resources of Catholic education should be concentrated on direct aid to the poor (with a probable cutback in services to white, middle-class Catholics) or on raising the level of social consciousness and commitment among the predominantly middle-class white students whom it now serves. Although this appears to be an either/or proposition, it is much more likely to be settled on a both/and basis: that is, although there should be a substantial increase in the commitment of Catholic education to the disadvantaged, a massive reduction in programs for white, middle-class Catholics is neither likely nor desirable. For one thing, it is becoming increasingly doubtful just how much white educators, whether from the public or nonpublic sector, can expect to accomplish among the predominantly black residents of the inner city. Like it or not, the current mood among black people is to resist the efforts of white "outsiders." The militant black community wants to help itself, not to be helped. And Catholic education, all too regrettably, is still largely a white enterprise, sponsored and staffed by white people and thus likely to encounter formidable obstacles in the ghetto. At the very least, white educators—and not just those who are Catholic—must undergo a fundamental change of attitude if they are to be effective in the black community. Not long ago a black Catholic priest was asked whether in his opinion there was any longer a place for white priests in ghetto parishes. "There's a place for them," he said, "and we'll be glad to have them—provided they think black." The same formula, "think black," seems relevant for white educators trying to define their new role in the black community.

A new phenomenon in the American educational scene is the "community school," either publicly owned, with policy set by the local community, or privately owned and operated by a closed corporation. Either way, the purpose is to meet, more directly than other schools have done, the needs of the community it serves. Pioneering storefront academies, such as Harlem Prep in New York (a college-oriented school for dropouts) and the Store Front Learning Center in Boston, have demonstrated what can be accomplished. Now "community" schools are beginning to spring up in what were formerly Catholic parochial schools. Among the pioneers are St. Patrick's Urban Community School in Cleveland, the Queen of Angels School in Newark and St. Paul's School in Baltimore. Such a development seems logical for many inner-city areas, where a heavy percentage of the children enrolled in parochial schools are non-Catholic. Catholic schools may also find themselves nudged in this direction by "purchase-of-service" school aid legislation like that enacted in 1968 and 1969 by Pennsylvania, Connecticut and other states.

Even so, there is still the question whether a massive reorientation of the Catholic school effort toward the inner city would be in the best interests of society. If one accepts, even partially, the conclusion of the National Advisory Commission on Civil Disorders that white racism is the central factor in the current urban crisis, it would seem to follow that education with a social conscience should now concentrate its chief energies on changing white attitudes. Here Catholic education can and should play an important role, since in many big cities of the North some of the most rabid anti-Negro sentiment is being expressed among white ethnic groups that are traditionally Catholic. Converting these people (or at least their sons and daughters), to a Christian view of racial relations might in the long run be the greatest contribution Catholic schools could make toward solving the problem of white racism. Of the new priorities that are called for in Catholic education, it is our belief that this should be the first. Catholic schools in the inner city *should* be strengthened: they should have the best administrators, the best teachers, the best facilities and equipment, and the most generous financial support (which inevitably will mean large diocesan subsidies). At the same time, Catholic schools cannot afford to turn their backs on their traditional white clientele, for the simple reason that in doing so they would be abandoning their best hope for a long-range contribution toward solving the racial crisis. As Bishop Ernest J. Primeau of Manchester, New Hampshire, has put it:

> Solutions will not come about . . . by concentrating on only one segment of American society. Obviously vastly more must be done—in education as in other fields—for the poor and the disadvantaged, the direct victims of discrimination. But more must also be done to change the attitudes of middle-class Americans and convince them of their responsibility to their less fortunate brothers. In essence, this is an educational task. Catholic education need not apologize for including the middle-class among those whom it serves. The question is not *whether* we should be teaching white middle-class Catholics, but *what* we should be teaching them. The issue, in my mind, comes down to this: Are we preparing white Catholic Americans to fit into American society—or are we preparing them to change American society by infusing it with the values of justice and charity to all men?

The response of "white" Catholic schools to the nation's racial crisis must involve, among other things, a determined effort to eliminate every vestige of racial separatism from their classrooms. It is not enough merely to adopt a policy of open admission; on the contrary, positive steps need to be taken to end *de facto* segregation. Black students and teachers should be actively recruited for Catholic schools, especially secondary institutions, and where necessary the ghetto youths should be given financial assistance and remedial in-

struction to compensate for their disadvantaged backgrounds. At lower levels, programs of transporting students in order to achieve a racial "mix" should be undertaken where feasible. Negro history and culture should be
made a part of the Catholic school curriculum—as has been
done, for example, in Catholic elementary and secondary
schools throughout the state of Michigan under a program
approved by the diocesan superintendents. Some idea of the
thrust of the program is conveyed by this passage from a
sixth-grade unit on Africa developed for schools in the Lan-
sing diocese:

> There will be several experiences in African music and
> art while the unit is in process. . . . The children will
> study religion in Africa—its impact upon culture and cus-
> tom for the people of Africa. There will be two class peri-
> ods in the physical education program when the children
> will appreciate dance and games of Africa. The literature
> class will devote three periods to the study of African
> fairy tales and how they reflect many of the things that
> they have learned about the people, their religious and po-
> litical attitudes, their history, etc.

Pupil- and teacher-exchange programs between suburban
and inner-city schools should be adopted. In short, for the
sake of both black and white students, Catholic schools
must do everything in their power to remove every trace of
practical racism; otherwise, all the talk about "values," so
far as racial justice is concerned, will be no more than talk.

These proposals for the Catholic school of the future may
seem unrealistic, at a time when Catholic schools are faced
with the basic problems of survival. How can their service
be expanded when there are fewer schools? The answer is
simple, although for some it will be painful: Catholic
schools can no longer measure success in numbers but only
in quality. However many or few Catholic schools there

may be in the future, in every aspect of their programs they must be distinguished by excellence. It is manifestly impossible today to enroll every American Catholic child in a Catholic school. Thus Catholic schools have to define their purposes clearly, and the starting point for such a definition must be quality: in personnel, in academic program, and above all in results. It may be that in thus defining their goals, the Catholic schools will have written themselves out of the picture so far as a segment of the Catholic community is concerned. It remains to be seen whether Catholic schools that emphasize commitment to racial justice, the eradication of poverty, and equal distribution of the goods of the earth among the peoples of the earth will command the support of the same clientele as in the past. But it may be that they will—that precisely this sort of education is what more and more Christian parents will be seeking for their children. But in any event, Catholic schools cannot afford to compromise their goals simply to stay in business. They will accomplish far more in the long run by serving the students (and the parents) who share their commitment than by attempting to please a clientele whose values run more or less counter to it. Among the latter, influences at home will tend to undermine the aims of the school, and thus the cards will be stacked against its succeeding. In part, however, the problem of conflicting parental attitudes will become less acute as the schools broaden their scope to encompass the education of the total Christian community. Without abandoning their commitment to the young, the schools must also make their facilities and their faculties available for the education of adults and of children not in Catholic schools. This will mean the creative development of new programs and the use of new media, but it will be worth the effort. In this way Catholic schools may be able to extend their service even as their numbers decline.

Structures for the Future

Goals are useless without the means of achieving them. Neither phasing-out nor business-as-usual can be the policy of Catholic schools in the future. There must be a drastic restructuring to bring them into harmony with the contemporary needs of the Church and of society.

If the Catholic school system in its present form did not exist, it is unlikely that anyone would now be calling for its establishment. This is not to condemn the past; and certainly it does not mean that the effort poured into Catholic schools over the past hundred years has been wasted. What it does mean, quite simply, is that the America of 1970 is a very different place from the America of 1870, and the structure that was built up in the closing years of the nineteenth century is inadequate for the closing decades of the twentieth.

The reasons for this are not merely theoretical. Nothing is more obvious in American education today than that first-rate schools cost a great deal of money. Improved physical facilities, new educational hardware such as computers and audiovisual equipment, higher salaries for teachers—all these are now components of first-class education, and Catholic schools are under the same pressure as the rest to provide them. They are what parents demand and what students deserve. But small, isolated institutions will find it increasingly difficult—and eventually impossible—to pay for them. If these schools are to compete in the educational marketplace of the immediate future, they must start looking now for the means of doing so.

Merger and consolidation are essential to the restructuring of Catholic education today. For better or worse, mergers are now inescapably part of the American economic scene, simply because they make sense administratively and financially. The corner grocery store is replaced by the supermarket; the independent book publisher is bought up by the diversified giant corporation. In education the neighborhood school is challenged by the "educational park" concept. It would be short-sighted and tragically unrealistic to suppose that Catholic schools, if they are to survive, can stand apart as bastions of autonomy.

Thus, first of all Catholic schools—in many places, if not everywhere—must be removed from the parochial structure. "Catholic school" must no longer be synonymous with "parochial school." In some dioceses and sections of the country, to be sure, parochial education still makes sense; (but these, too, will be the better for a dose of streamlining and centralization in such matters as academic standards and financing). But in many other places, "parochial" education years ago ceased to make sense. Where that is so, the fact has to be faced and the structure changed.

The reasons for cutting the school loose from the parish are often compelling. In many areas, particularly older city parishes, parish population—and with it, school enrollment—has dropped sharply in recent years. Elsewhere, especially in rural areas, the enrollment in individual parish schools has never been very high. But today the effort to operate a comprehensive elementary school (grades one to eight) for a very small student body is wasteful of resources and is likely to have mediocre results as well. The problem is only sharpened by the soaring cost of education and by the dropoff in religious vocations (and thus of available religious teachers). In many areas factors like these have made the parish school a dubious luxury whose continued existence is far from certain.

The numerous advantages of consolidation include eliminating two-grade classrooms, the possibility of improved instructional techniques such as departmentalization and team teaching, and the pooling of library and audiovisual resources. Teachers with special skills in particular subjects are able to concentrate on what they do best, and at the same time reach more children.

Naturally, there are practical drawbacks such as the transportation problem, but these are seldom beyond solution. A more real difficulty is the reluctance of pastors and parishioners to lose the close identification of parish and school to which they have been accustomed. Yet most Catholic secondary schools long ago moved out of the parish structure, and there is no intrinsic reason why elementary schools cannot now do the same. Severing the link between the parish and the school may hurt at first, but in the long run it offers perhaps the best formula for keeping Catholic schools a going concern.

How would consolidation work? Under a typical plan, four neighboring parishes, each of whose schools at present offers a comprehensive program from grades one through eight, might join forces. School "A" might become a nongraded school for children of preschool age plus grades one through four, school "B" a middle school offering departmental instruction, and school "C" a resource center providing special services, CCD programs and adult education facilities, with school "D," whose physical plant is inadequate or in bad repair, to be closed down entirely.

Such a plan would need cooperation among the pastors, the parish boards of education (where these exist), and the religious communities who staff the schools involved. Funds would be pooled, transportation plans would be developed jointly, and teachers of different communities would teach side by side in the same school. All this runs contrary to the pattern of isolation and noncommunication that has prevailed in Catholic schools. But this pattern, always indefensible, now becomes dangerous folly.

Such a program would also require a degree of planning and coordination at the diocesan level that up to now has seldom been evident. A diocesan planning group could set up teaching teams, to be rotated among a number of schools —an approach that is especially well suited to religious education, where master teachers have always been in particular demand. One can envision such diocesan teams serving schools, CCD classes and adult education groups, with invigorating results for them all.

One practical result of such coordination would be to open up Catholic schools—and school personnel—to the possibility of serving other groups within the Catholic and general communities besides those they have reached hitherto. The school would become a resource not just for its students but for adults and CCD youngsters as well. The wasteful current practice of using school facilities for only a few hours a day, five days a week, would be eliminated, as better planning made it possible to put the schools to use in the evenings and on weekends. School personnel would be given the opportunity to participate in these added programs. Many sisters, for example, would welcome the experience of instructing adults as well as children. The idea, of course, is not to get extra mileage out of the teachers by working them overtime, but rather, by imaginative planning and scheduling—as, for example, in the use of rotating teams on a diocesan or regional basis—to make possible a broader role without overburdening them.

Another area for innovation is in coordinating the home and the school. Studies like that by Greeley and Rossi underline the pivotal role of the home in forming the values of the young. The school, Greeley and Rossi write, "can indeed make a substantial contribution to the development of value-oriented behavior patterns, but it can do so only when the values of the school are reinforced in the family environment. . . . A combination of Catholic education and parental devotion produces a remarkably high level of religious behavior in adult life."

But even though it is obvious that home and school

should work together closely, up to now little or nothing has been done to bring the two into a systematic relationship. Indeed, the best that was usually hoped for was that the home and the school would not work at cross purposes. A new arrangement is needed now to bring school and family together in a program that stresses value formation. Catholic education, the rationale for whose existence is the inculcation of values, must use all its skill in developing experimental and innovative programs for this purpose.

How might an experimental Catholic school that took this important factor into consideration be expected to function? Clearly, there can be no set formula; an experiment in education, as in anything else, must leave room for flexibility, for shifts in emphasis, for the abandonment of one approach in favor of another that may be new and untried. As a means of enlisting the family in the process of formal education, the school might provide tape recordings to be played at home. After listening to the tape, together or separately, the parents and children would discuss its contents. The project might deal with the liturgy and liturgical changes, or with such matters as race relations, the morality of war, or the problem of poverty in an affluent society. The family discussion could provide feedback to the schools in the form of student reports, and lead eventually to school-sponsored action programs.

Clearly there are potential difficulties in such an approach —if, for instance, the school made the mistake of seeming to patronize the parents or to place them on the same level of intellectual and emotional development as their children. But this difficulty could be avoided if it were made clear that the school regarded the parents as co-educators. Here the intelligence and tact that went into preparing and presenting the material for family discussion would be all-important, as would the readiness of the school to accept and act upon feedback from the family.

Recent years have seen increased emphasis on guidance and counseling in education. At present, however, most of this activity takes place within the confines of the school; illogical as it may seem (since counseling is essentially a function of mental health), parents are seldom brought into the picture. The experimental Catholic school could remedy this situation by arranging home conferences with counselors and other school personnel. Such counseling would become a bridge between school and home—and a major factor in the formation of values.

More cooperation with public schools should be another objective in the restructuring of Catholic schools. There has, for example, been much talk in recent years about the possibility of educational parks—school enclaves designed to serve entire metropolitan areas, to break down *de facto* segregation based on housing patterns, and provide high-quality educational facilities. Catholic school people should be active in developing these projects long before they get past the drawing board, by remaining alert to ways in which Catholic education can contribute to the enterprise. Such parks might, for example, include Catholic education centers, operating under a "shared-time" arrangement. To be sure, shared time generally has been regarded by Catholics as a mere stopgap, an expedient designed solely to keep the wolf from the door. In an educational park, however, shared time could well become a creative means of bringing the best in Catholic schooling to the largest number of Catholic students, while at the same time fostering ecumenical and civic unity.

Along with other schools, too, Catholic schools must give serious weight to the criticism by psychologists of traditional educational practice. It is becoming clear, for instance, that a lockstep organization by "grades" is based on a totally unrealistic assumption about how children learn—namely that after nine months, no more and no less, of exposure to certain material, all the children in a group will be ready to move ahead. Possibly the most important educational development in recent years has been the individualization of instruction, gearing it to the mental and emotional development of the child and giving him opportunity to follow whatever avenues may appeal to his special tastes and abilities. This is not the place for detailed discussion of these and other innovative practices; but it is clear that the Catholic school of the future must, along with other schools of quality, be able to provide its students the joy that arises from self-realization and self-fulfillment.

The new educational methods reflect, as often as not, more than a tinkering with the mechanics of instruction, but a whole new vision of what and how and why students do and should learn. Among the schools in this country that have made a thoroughgoing commitment to experiment and innovation is Chaminade High School in Dayton, Ohio, operated by the Marianists for the archdiocese of Cincinnati.

In September 1969, after several years of tentative experiment in various departments, Chaminade launched a radically altered program emphasizing student freedom. Class attendance was made optional; the number of examinations was reduced, and they were shortened in length; students were encouraged to evaluate their own progress, and it was decided to rate no student in any course a "failure" (on the theory that to do so is to inflict a needless blow on the student's self-esteem). Classrooms became "student-centered" rather than "teacher-centered." The major thrust of education was toward developing skills rather than accumulating specific information (so much of which is soon out of date in today's fast-changing world). The objective of these and other innovations is to encourage self-directed learning and a responsible, orderly and self-disciplined use of freedom.

Such a program may sound neither feasible nor desirable

to more tradition-minded educators, alumni and parents. Yet it reflects the eagerness of some contemporary educators to find better ways of preparing today's students for life in the world of tomorrow. More and more Catholic schools are experiencing this restlessness and this willingness to experiment.

Accountability

If Catholic schools are to open out into new cooperation with public schools, and into the expanded service of groups both within and outside the Catholic community, they must accept the principle of accountability. We have already referred to the economic aspects of this in our chapter on financing. As a matter of justice, Catholic schools must answer, in candid detail, for the use they make of the money entrusted to them. And if they are to receive expanded support from public funds, such accountability becomes not merely desirable but mandatory.

The concept of accountability, however, goes beyond economic matters. It means that Catholic schools must be answerable in the broadest sense to the public—or rather, the publics—they serve. Educators often tend to isolate themselves behind a barricade of bureaucracy and jargon in order to carry on their business—often with the best of intentions, but in general pretty much as they like. This state of affairs is intolerable in any school system, but is particularly so in Catholic schools, which exist to serve the Church and society and to continue the educational effort of the home.

Boards of education, as we have seen, offer one highly effective means of ensuring the accountability of the Catholic school. A board functioning as it should is truly a voice of the community, through which public sentiment is conveyed to the professional educators. In any such body, however, there is a tendency to wall itself off from the community it is supposed to represent. The Catholic board of education movement needs to guard against this danger. Its members must be careful to avoid any of the "us-and-them" mentality that would divorce it from community concerns.

Important as it is, the board is thus only one instrument for guaranteeing accountability on the part of the school. Other structures need to be developed as well. The challenge is particularly acute in the area of religious education, where Catholic schools are feeling the results of deterioration in the social and even the doctrinal consensus among American Catholics. This is apparent from the controversies that have erupted in Catholic schools over the use of textbooks containing praise of civil rights leaders such as Martin Luther King, Jr., or the introduction of sex education programs. Applying the principle of accountability in such situations becomes extremely difficult. It cannot be equated with capitulation—as would have happened, for instance, if a school de-emphasized civil rights because of protests from a bigoted majority. But neither can the school administration sail straight ahead, self-righteously ignoring the wishes of parents and the community. Instead, the parents and the other members of the community have to be actively involved in planning school programs (as has been done, for instance, in the archdiocese of Cincinnati), and provision needs to be made for a continuing give-and-take and exchange of views—itself a form of education—between educators and the community they serve.

This will be particularly necessary as Catholic schools expand their service to the black community and to other minority groups. The struggle over community control now tormenting the public schools will sooner or later be a threat to Catholic schools as well. Catholic educators should learn from the problems of public education and develop such structures as community advisory councils, to provide the ghetto community with a degree of true control over school programs.

New goals and new structures: these are twin needs of Catholic schools at the present time. In developing them, the objective must be to broaden rather than narrow the scope of Catholic education. Ways must be found of serving new groups in the Church and society. Above all, the emphasis must be on instilling in young people a permanent sense of apostolic commitment that will make them leaders in the rebuilding of society. If Catholic schools can do this, it will be proof that they have not outlived their usefulness, but indeed have scarcely begun to realize their potential for good.

We hear, these days, of crisis everywhere: in international affairs, in the cities, and in the churches too. It is thus not at all surprising that Catholic education should likewise find itself in that state. Although crisis is often thought of as synonymous with disaster, it need not be so. Granted, crisis can be the prelude to disaster; but essentially it is a sign of movement and of transition. Thus, while crisis may be a prelude to collapse, it is also the essential precondition of growth. This is true of individuals, whose progress toward maturity is signaled by successive crises of growth. It is also true of institutions and communities, whose adaptation to meet new challenges is always accompanied by strain and even anguish.

The essential difference between the crisis that is a mark of growth and the crisis that precedes disaster lies above all in the response of those who make it their task to face and cope with the need for change. For there is no doubt that crisis entails a challenge, a test of courage and imagination. It brings out the best in people, and it can also bring out the worst. In the nature of things, the resolution of a crisis is necessarily not predetermined. Its outcome depends on the human heart and the human will.

Catholic education today is at such a turning point. Indeed, Catholic education is faced with a multiplicity of crises—in finance, in personnel, and in the question of goals and priorities. It is possible to suppose that these problems are insoluble, and that the crisis has already sounded a death knell for the entire system of Catholic education. This we do not accept. We do not regard the problems that now confront Catholic education as beyond solution. Solutions may be difficult, they may be painful, they may not be wholly satisfactory; but they are not impossible. With intelligence, imagination and courage, the problems of Catholic education can be solved. The present crisis can become an avenue of growth and progress. The opportunity is there, and where there is opportunity there is also duty.